9/3/72

Dear Sura,

I picked this book for your birthday for several reasons. 1) You love jewelley. I think this book contains photos of the epitome of inlaid craftsmanship. 2) When you look at this book think of the precision involved and the patience it must have taken to make each piece. 3) The jewelley was worn by people who had a lot of leisure time. The reason, or part of it, was that Jews were slaving for them. 4) Be thankful that the skill and technical know how that is exhibited here is not in evidence in the present Egyptian hierarchy.
Happy Birthday.

Love Peter.

EGYPTIAN JEWELLERY

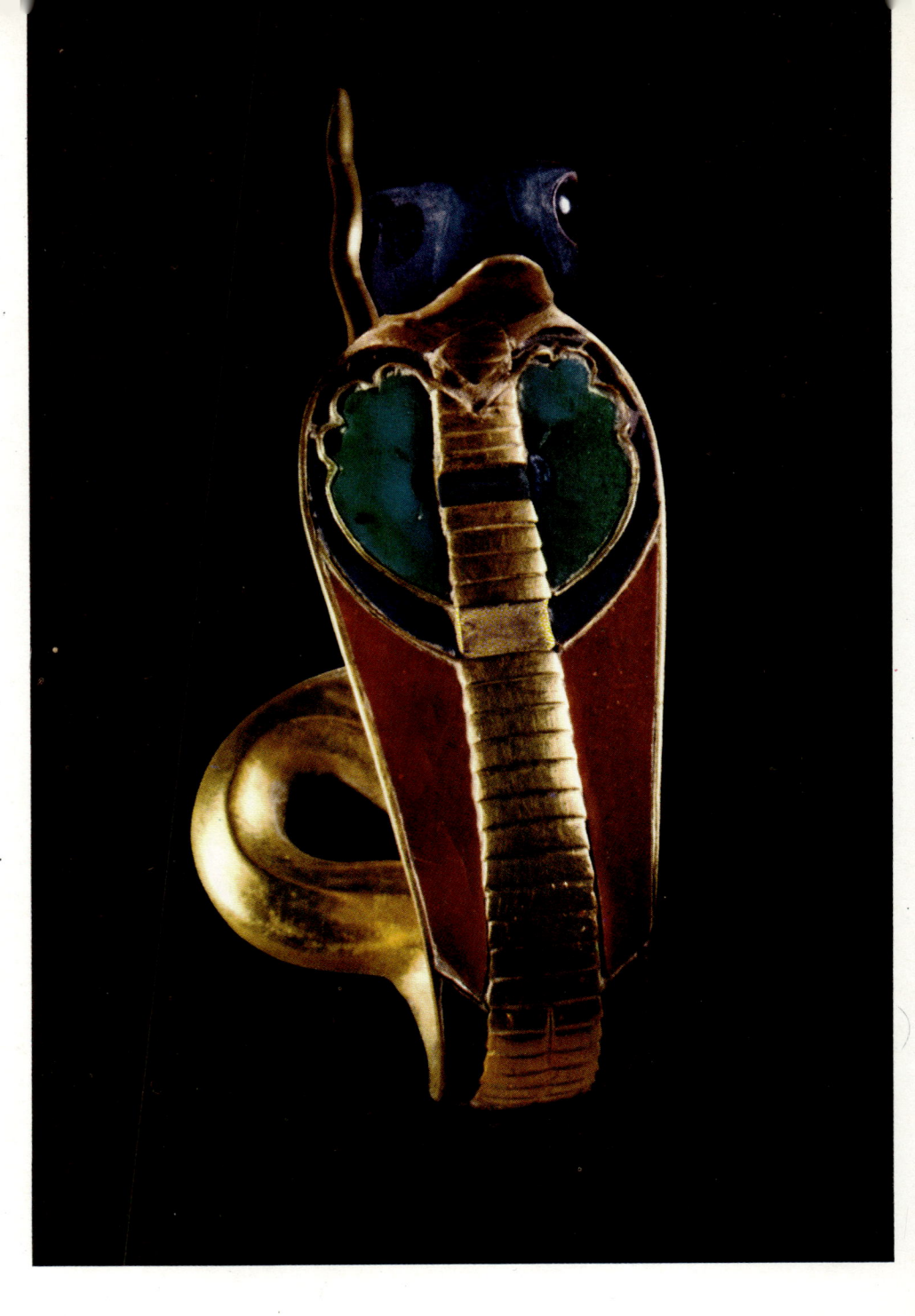

EGYPTIAN JEWELLERY

Text by Milada Vilímková
Selection of Illustration by Moh. H. Abdul-Rahman
Photography by Dominique Darbois

PAUL HAMLYN

LONDON · NEW YORK · SYDNEY · TORONTO

TEXT BY MILADA VILÍMKOVÁ
SELECTION OF ILLUSTRATIONS
BY MOH. H. ABDUL-RAHMAN
PHOTOGRAPHED BY DOMINIQUE DARBOIS
TRANSLATED BY IRIS URWIN
DESIGNED BY KAREL PÁNEK

DESIGNED AND PRODUCED BY ARTIA FOR
THE HAMLYN PUBLISHING GROUP LIMITED
LONDON · NEW YORK · SYDNEY · TORONTO
Hamlyn House, Feltham, Middlesex, England

© 1969 by ARTIA
PRINTED IN CZECHOSLOVAKIA BY SVOBODA, PRAGUE
S—2358

ACKNOWLEDGEMENTS

My thanks are due to Professor Jaroslav Černý of Oxford University and to Miss Helen Murray of the Griffith Institute of the Ashmolean Museum, Oxford, for their very great kindness in providing information on the jewels from the tomb of Tutankhamūn. I am also grateful to Dr. Miroslav Verner for his help and advice while I was working in the library of the Czechoslovak Egyptological Institute.

Milada Vilímková

LIST OF CONTENTS

I	The Beginnings	9
II	The Protodynastic Period	12
III	The Old Kingdom	15
IV	The Middle Kingdom	20
V	The New Kingdom	28
VI	The Late Dynastic Period	40
VII	The End of Egyptian Tradition	42
VIII	Decoration in Egyptian Jewellery	45
IX	Materials and Techniques	49

List of Abbreviations used in the Notes	52
Notes	53
Illustrations and Catalogue	57
Chronological Table	135
List of Illustrations	137

I

THE BEGINNINGS

The long development of ancient Egyptian jewellery started far back in prehistoric times, in small settlements and graves on the edge of the Nile valley, particularly in Upper Egypt. Finds from this era have been assigned by archaeologists to the neolithic and chalcolithic periods, the latter covering the Badarian civilization (named from the main source of the finds, Badāri), and the Amratian and Gerzean civilizations.[1] These were followed by the first dynasties, the age known as the protodynastic period.

Personal adornment is one of the oldest and most fundamental needs of man, and it is not surprising to find things which served this purpose even in neolithic settlements, for example, at Merimda on the edge of the Libyan Desert, and in the oasis of Fayūm. The most frequent finds are beads which undoubtedly formed necklaces or bracelets; pendants, which may have been used as early as this, as protective amulets; bracelets and even rings. The materials are of many different kinds: coloured stones, ivory, bone, shell and clay, smoothed and baked. Although the types of ornament are relatively numerous, the execution is extremely primitive. The beads, cylindrical or disk-shaped, are often irregular; a roughly dressed stone with a hole bored through it suffices as a pendant; the ivory rings are sometimes decorated with a small boss; a simple band ring of ivory serves as a bracelet.[2]

The range of jewellery found in graves of the Badarian civilization is similar: beads, pendants and bracelets. The beads are mainly made of stone, soft steatite is a favourite, often with a turquoise coloured glaze; of the harder stones, the semi-precious cornelian, jasper and turquoise are used. Ivory and shells are made into beads, too; so is ostrich egg-shell, and even dried clay, coloured red. Most of the beads are cylindrical-, barrel- or disk-shaped. Pendants are geometrically shaped, or are very primitive formalized animals made out of the same materials as the beads. Necklaces, bracelets and belts are made of shells strung together, as well as of beads; the shells come mostly from the shores of the Red Sea. Judging from the position in which the jewellery was found in the graves, necklaces, bracelets and belts are the most usual forms of adornment, although head ornaments and anklets also exist. Bracelets, besides being made of beads, are sometimes solid bands of ivory, tortoise-shell or horn, occasionally decorated with a raised boss or an engraved design of dots.[3] These ornaments are also shown on the female figurines of the period: the fired clay figure found at Badāri has a necklace of large beads painted in black round its neck.[4]

The types of jewellery found in graves of the Amratian civilization do not differ from those of the previous period, except that metal, gold and copper is used. The first examples of faience, glazed earthenware, also appear, a material characteristic of Egyptian applied art under all the dynasties. The animal shaped pendants, such as the faience bird found in a grave in Naqāda, are already much more recognizable.[5] Ivory bracelets are again common, with rarer examples made of shell or tortoise-shell, or of alabaster or flint. The rings, which are much rarer, are decorated with a raised boss, or even with a more elaborate design, like that on the ivory band ring shaped like two lions facing each other, found at Naqāda.[6] No anklets have been found in the graves, although some of the female figurines of the period have painted ones.

The basic types of jewellery remain unchanged in the succeeding period, that of the Gerzean civilization, but the choice of material is wider; it now includes more semi-precious stones and other coloured pebbles, and also, occasionally, silver. Soft steatite covered with a coloured glaze is still used and faience occurs in greater quantity. There are a large number of pendants, some of them in geometrical shapes, others in the shape of common things of daily use, such as pitchers or cosmetic palettes, and, as in the previous periods, shaped like animals or parts of an animal. They include lions, jackals, crocodiles, frogs, flies, hawks, heads of oxen and birds, and the occasional fantastic composite, such as a four-legged animal with a hawk's head.[7] Beads and seashells are strung together to make necklaces, bracelets and belts, and more rarely fillets. In some cases the component beads have been found still lying in their original position on the dead body, although the ornament itself had fallen to pieces; reconstruction is thus not difficult. A few of the pieces already show an attempt to integrate different elements in a single design; the fillet found in grave no. 1730 in Abydos is designed in four units, with rows of gold beads separated by rows of garnet, turquoise and glazed steatite beads.[8] Strings of beads of the same material were also found. Oval pendants, sometimes slightly concave, appear for the first time in this period; these Sir Flinders Petrie thought had probably been worn on the brow, held in place by a ribbon or a single string of beads. They are mostly made of sea-shells, and more rarely of horn, stone, copper or gold.[9]

It is clear from this brief survey of the jewellery worn before the dynastic period that the articles of adornment commonly found today, in particular necklaces, bracelets and rings, are already constant features; while fillets, anklets and ornamental belts are somewhat less common. Nothing which requires piercing the body has been found, no ear- or nose-rings. Ancient jewellery is mostly very simple ornament and fundamentally natural.

The only materials preserved in these prehistoric graves are substances like stone, metal, ivory, horn, shell, which do not suffer at all, or only relatively little, from the effects of time and atmosphere. There can be no doubt, however, that among the oldest adornments of man were fresh flowers; indeed wreaths or necklaces of flowers may have been even older than necklaces of beads, shells, or teeth and claws of wild animals. The variety of shape, colour and scent of flowers must have had the same attraction for man in ancient times as today. The art of making wreaths of flowers, handed down from generation to generation, is one at which every child born in the country is adept. Wreaths have been found in Egyptian tombs, but they are, of course, of a later period.[10] It is possible that this all too short-lived form of adornment was not originally a part of funeral furniture, and for this reason prehistoric tombs do not provide us with evidence of its use. Formalized flower motifs, however, are found in jewellery of the earliest dynasties. If at this early stage flowers are imitated in more lasting materials, the people of the Nile valley must have used flowers for their personal decoration long before.

The jewels and articles of adornment found in Egyptian graves of the predynastic period are a very simple collection of stones of many colours given a more or less basic shape and a hole for threading them, sea-shells, larger and smaller bands of ivory, stone and other materials, beads, rings of gold, silver and copper, and pendants in geometrical or formalized natural shapes. With the addition of fresh flowers, the foundations on which the art of the later Egyptian jewellers was laid had already made their appearance.

II

THE PROTODYNASTIC PERIOD

In the protodynastic period the direction of the future development of the art of Egyptian jewellery can already be seen. Although the basic choice of coloured stones and semi-precious stones never really changes, a preference for red cornelian and pale blue or green turquoise, or faience and steatite with a turquoise glaze gradually appears in this period. Pendants, both geometrical and animal, become more definite in outline.[1] Ivory bracelets become flatter, broader, and the outer surface is often decorated with two or three horizontal, rounded bands separated by grooves; or, as in the fragments from the First Dynasty royal tombs in Abydos, they are engraved with rows of diamond-shaped quadrangles separated by zigzag patterns, with bands of zigzag ornament, or simple interlacing patterns.[2] All these ornamental motifs, particularly the combination of diamonds with zigzag patterns, are much more widely used later. The diamond and zigzag pattern is for a long time a characteristic feature of the ornamental belts, which are so specifically Egyptian. It appears for the first time at a very early date on the king's belt in the famous palette of king Narmer. Ceremonial palettes, which developed from the flat stone tables used for crushing cosmetics, served as vehicles for decoration. It is difficult to say whether the particular belt shown on Narmer's palette was made by a jeweller or woven or plaited like a mat. Indeed much of the evidence for the long use of this pattern is gained indirectly, as here, from reliefs and paintings rather than the original objects. The scenes depicted on Narmer's palette are interesting from another point of view as well; the bearer of the king's sandals wears a large amulet on his breast shaped rather like the 'enclosed' pectorals (pendant ornaments worn on the breast) which have survived from a much later period. On the other side of the palette the same official is wearing a bird-shaped amulet very similar to the ivory amulet found in one of the Abusīr tombs.[3]

Although they play little part in future development, from the artistic point of view, the most notable pieces of jewellery of the protodynastic period are four bracelets found by Petrie at the beginning of this century in the tomb of king Djer at Abydos *(plates 1—4)*.[4] All four are of gold set with semi-precious stones, most important of which are the pale blue-green turquoise, dark blue lapis lazuli and purple amethyst.

On the second bracelet *(plate 2)* the gold and turquoise plaques representing archaic palace façade *serekh* with the falcon of Horus perched on it, are most remarkable. The gold and turquoise plaques alternate, becoming smaller towards the end, and are finished off with a triangular gold fastening. This repetition of the same motif in two colours is typical of Egyptian decoration. Nevertheless Petrie thought that this treatment was not the original one. On the turquoise plaques the falcons are archaic in form, with somewhat hunched bodies, while those on the gold plaques are upright. This would suggest that the original bracelet of turquoise plaques was damaged and repaired at a later date with gold plaques bearing a similar motif. A bracelet of a similar type but less precious, being in faience, dating from only slightly later (the reign of king Djer), was found at Gīza.[5] The plaques in this case are separated by two beads; unlike those in the king Djer bracelet they are not arranged in one direction, but are placed symmetrically round an axis, so that eight of the thirteen hawks are facing left while the remaining five are facing right. This led Petrie to suggest that three plaques may be missing.

An interesting feature of the first bracelet *(plate 1)* is the central gold rosette, shaped like a flower with small petals turned inwards, and accompanied by a symmetrical arrangement of turquoise and gold beads in threes. This is the first example of a formal flower motif in Egyptian jewellery. The fourth bracelet *(plate 4)* is also designed with a symmetrical arrangement of threes, but there is no emphasis on a central motif. There are two alternating motifs on the third bracelet *(plate 3)*: three double beads of gold and amethyst, attached by a wire in a groove down the centre, and two rhomboid turquoise beads in gold facing formed by biconical gold tubes joined end to end at their narrowest point.

The falcon of Horus on the façade of the royal palace seems to have been a popular motif, indeed one of the most frequently used, for, beside the two bracelets mentioned here, single plaques of ivory and lapis lazuli of the same shape have been found[6] and it occurs commonly on cylinder seals. There is an interesting use, reminiscent of three of the Djer bracelets, of arrangements of differently-shaped beads in the row of necklaces painted in black and red on a fragment of a wooden figure of a man from Abydos.[7] In two of the necklaces elongated barrel-shaped beads alternate *(a-b)* with small spherical ones; in another, large olive-shaped beads with a trace of spiral engraving alternate with small smooth beads of the same shape and small spheres, in a more complicated system. Petrie thought that this may have been a representation of gold beads made of spirally twisted gold wire, like those used on the fourth bracelet from king Djer's tomb. Both the bracelets and these painted necklaces show the rich and original inventive powers of the jewellers of the early dynastic period, as well as their skill; it is sad that they only form a small part of what must have actually been made.[8]

In an enormous number of the tombs in predynastic burial grounds the funeral furniture was discovered intact; and, though rich in itself, it is modest in terms of the material used. Often it is possible to reconstruct with certainty even the order in which the beads had been threaded on strings long since turned to dust.

However, in the dynastic era the situation is different. The attitude of the ancient Egyptians to the after-life is well known; to ensure continued life in the next world it was not only necessary to prevent the decay of the dead body, but also to surround the dead man with everything he had been used to in his daily life, and which he would therefore need in the life to come. Jewellery was already in the predynastic era the most valuable personal property, worn on many occasions in private life and taken to the grave. The choice of material depended on the wealth of the owner, and the rulers and their families wore most valuable objects. With increasing power and higher position the quality and quantity of the funeral furniture rose, too. On the other hand, desire for gold was strong; from the time of the first dynasties it caused men to break with the very foundations of Egyptian religion. The tombs, which were built at enormous expense and provided with the maximum of cunning protection, nevertheless proved easy prey to the persistence of the robbers. The secret passages into the pyramids were discovered, the heavy stone sarcophagi broken open, and the carefully wrapped mummies of the rulers robbed of all their jewels and damaged, or even broken into pieces and carried off. There is hardly a single tomb where first in ancient and then in more modern times thieves had not been active before the archaeologists arrived. Only exceptional circumstances or chance have protected some royal mummies and funeral furniture from destruction, to remain intact for modern archaeologists. The collections of Egyptian jewellery in the Cairo Museum; the Metropolitan Museum, New York; the Museum of Fine Arts, Boston; the British Museum, London; the Louvre, Paris; the Berlin Museum and many other places have only been saved by accident from the immense wealth originally placed in the pyramids, mastabas and rock tombs. The most magnificent examples of ancient Egyptian jewellery, those that were made for the great pharaohs, have been destroyed. The gold they were made of was melted down, the semi-precious stones taken from their settings, and the whole sold piece by piece.

This brings us to a question which has not yet received detailed study. We know that the gold-bearing region between the Nile valley and the Red Sea was extensive, and that gold was mined there in very early times. Later on gold was paid in tribute by the conquered peoples, particularly by the Nubians. We do not know, of course, how much was mined, and even if gold was imported into Egypt in considerable quantities during the New Kingdom. Nevertheless consumption must have been fantastically high. What then happened to the vast amounts of gold stolen from the tombs? The ordinary Egyptian could not wear royal jewels, nor would he have cared to. What he wanted to do was to change the gold and precious stones for something more useful. Since gold was not currency in our sense of the word, jewellers were the only people who could be interested in getting hold of it, for their wealthy, highly placed customers. We know from murals and carvings that rich Egyptians had their own private jewellers' workshops in their houses; and it can be assumed that such workshops existed at the royal court and were probably attached to the temples, too. In these circumstances it would not be the jewellers working in these shops who were anxious to get hold of gold, but the men in charge of them. Thus it is probable some of the gold that went into the jewellery of every Egyptian ruler and his family had been stolen from the tomb of one of their royal ancestors, although the direct robbery of one king's tomb by another was probably exceptional. The famous trial of robbers of the Twentieth Dynasty tombs almost gives the impression that their deed was condoned, as though it was assumed that the gold stolen from royal tombs would find its way by some circuitous route to another royal tomb. Nor is it impossible that the fact that Tutankhamūn's gold coffin was found may be directly connected with the absence of gold coffins for any of his predecessors.

III

THE OLD KINGDOM

Royal tombs became tremendously rich during the Old Kingdom, but, because of the widespread activities of robbers, relatively little jewellery has survived. Statues and reliefs provide additional information and from these two sources the nature of the jewellery popular during the period can be approximately determined.

From the well-known wooden steles carved in relief, in the tomb of Hesirē, it might be supposed that the men of the Third Dynasty were remarkably sober and scorned all personal adornment. It is likely, however, that the sculptor of these reliefs, an artist of exceptional talent, had his own reason for leaving out all lesser details. The carvings are certainly more effective for the lack of distracting descriptive detail. On the other hand, another nobleman called Khabausokar was portrayed, only a little later, in the relief carvings on the false doors of his mastaba in Saqqāra, wearing a remarkably complicated necklace which covers the whole of his chest.[1] The circle round his neck is joined by three serpentine bands to an elongated, fantastic animal, its forequarters bearing a jackal's head, human hands and a pair of hind legs which hang below one shoulder, while the hindquarters with four animal trotters hang below the other. The middle section of the piece is separated off by flat circular disks and a large ring. From Khabausokar's neck twelve separate strings hang in four sets one above the other with three amulets shaped like the hieroglyph *ankh*, three circular amulets, another three *ankh* amulets, and in the fourth row three more circular amulets. In their evaluation of the finds in Khabausokar's mastaba, M. A. Murray and K. Sethe came to the conclusion that this unusual ornament was the mark of a priest of the god Anubis. There is a similarly complicated necklace carved in relief on the fragments of a granite statue which is thought to be a later copy.[2]

The jewels discovered during the excavation of king Sekhemkhet's pyramid in 1951 are quite different.[3] They comprise a set of twenty-one slightly rounded gold band bracelets, and one composed of ten rows of spherical gold beads separated by strips of gold. Both these types are extremely interesting in the light of later developments. The gold bands, which are of graduated width, are undoubtedly the earliest examples of a type of bracelet seen frequently in reliefs of the Fourth and Fifth Dynasties, but certainly known as early as the end of the predynastic era. From iconographic evidence, it appears that sets of bracelets were worn only by women, on both arms, often covering the whole of their forearms. The second bracelet is an example of the bead bracelet with spacers which remained popular right up to the late dynastic period, while the sets of flat bands went out of fashion at the end of the Old Kingdom. The spacers later became part of the decoration, but in this one the strips of gold with holes for the single strands of the bracelet play no part in the design and are only there to keep the beads a certain distance apart. This, too, was women's jewellery, for judging from the figures in mural paintings and reliefs, men did not wear this kind of bracelet until a much later period. The sarcophagus in the undisturbed pyramid chamber was empty when found. This mystery, whether such distinctly feminine jewellery could have been part of king Sekhemkhet's funeral furniture, or whether his queen was to have been buried in the pyramid he had built, are puzzles which are unlikely ever to be solved.

Rather more is known about the different types of jewels worn in the Fourth, Fifth and Sixth Dynasties, although the original pieces have rarely survived. The famous statue of princess Nofret in the Cairo Museum gives us an idea of what an elegant Egyptian woman wore under the Fourth Dynasty. On a wig of cleverly plaited locks, which covered the princess' own hair completely, is a fillet — a band of white ornamented with symmetrical flower designs. In the centre of her brow there is an eight-part rosette with a black centre, and on either side are slender blue cup-shaped flowers with red centres, and attached to them red rosettes and another triple motif of blue rosettes and red flowers. Round her neck the princess is wearing a broad collar necklace of blue, green and red bands, of beads separated by narrower white bands and ending in a row of dark blue drop beads. Her wrists are hidden by the folds of her cloak, so that we cannot see the bracelets which she certainly wore in real life. The coloured ornament on a white ground was undoubtedly used by the artist to suggest a silver fillet with flower motifs set with cornelian, turquoise and lapis lazuli. The collar necklace was probably in reality made up of close rows of cylindrical beads of lapis lazuli, turquoise and cornelian, separated by rows of small beads of silver. The drop pendants may also have been set with lapis lazuli. Unlike the later fashion, princess Nofret's collar necklace goes high up her neck. Since her wig hides the back of her neck, the fastening of the necklace is hidden; it may still have been the archaic *nebyet*, identical to the hieroglyph for gold *(nebu)*, or the type which later became common, the *wesekh* ('the broad'). The fact that the rows of beads go so high up the neck would suggest the use of the older type fastened by means of circular disks holding the ribbons or strings on the nape of the neck. The top row was straight in the *nebyet* type, and therefore shorter; in the *wesekh* type it became a curved segment or semi-circle. The princess' husband, prince Rahotpe, is adorned with a single jewel, a dark amulet shaped like a five-lobed leaf, on a white cord.

From about the same time as this noble couple dates the valuable find, made by an American expedition led by G. A. Reisner in Gīza in 1925, of the undamaged tomb of queen Hetepheres, the mother of Khufu (Cheops).[4] This tomb presents a puzzle which archaeologists have not been able to solve completely. The tomb was intact when found, but the alabaster sarcophagus, which had seemed to offer the greatest promise, was empty. This astonishing fact can only be explained by the hypothesis that queen Hetepheres, wife of king Snofru, was originally buried near his pyramid in Dahshūr, and, probably fairly soon after her death, the tomb was robbed and the mummy stolen. Since the funeral furniture had otherwise not suffered much, the vizier may have kept silent about the loss and suggested moving the queen's tomb to the new burial ground in Gīza. Only an empty sarcophagus could, of course, be placed in the new tomb. Examination of the burial suggests that it was a cache rather than a typical tomb of the period — a mastaba with a structure built above the ground.

Among the funeral furniture, which has been systematically restored and reconstructed, is a wooden jewel-box covered in gold leaf, containing a set of twenty silver bracelets.[5] The bracelets are a particularly interesting find, as they provide information unavailable in paintings. They were slipped on to cylinders of wood and, judging from their increasing diameter, were meant for the forearm, which they would have covered from wrist to elbow. This is the same type of bracelet, therefore, as those found in king Sekhemkhet's pyramid, but consists of one pair less, as there is no doubt that the latter set was originally made up of twenty-two bracelets, although only twenty-one were found. Queen Hetepheres' bracelets, inlaid with lapis lazuli, cornelian and turquoise, have unique motifs consisting of alternating butterflies with their wings spread, and small roundels. The appearance of butterflies as early as the Old Kingdom refutes the previous theory that they did not occur until the Eighteenth Dynasty, under the influence of Aegean art. Leaving aside the fact that the Aegean formalization of the butterfly motif is somewhat different from this, it would be a bold assumption to make of such acute observers of nature as the Egyptians, that they had been unable to notice and depict a butterfly until Aegean art showed them how.[6]

The queen's jewel-box, covered with gold leaf both inside and out, is an interesting illustration of the greater value attached to silver than to gold in the period of the Old Kingdom. The combination on the bracelets of lapis lazuli and turquoise with silver looks cold and almost gloomy, and not even the details and the round disks inlaid in cornelian, between the butterflies, succeed in livening it up. The incrustation was not executed in the later cloisonné technique, but by cementing the stones into hollows cut in the metal. This way of stone-setting had been known in Egypt since the time of the earliest dynasties.[7]

The silver bracelets belonging to queen Hetepheres confirm the suggestion that the painted fillet on princess Nofret's statue was based on a silver original. This does not of course mean that silver had superseded gold. Several gold pieces have also been found.

When the burial ground of Gīza was excavated in 1931, the tomb of an unknown woman was discovered not far from the great sphinx; she was probably a princess, but as there are no inscriptions in the tomb we do not know her name.[8] The fillet worn by this princess is shown in plate 5. Similar is a fillet of copper and gilt wood found in Gīza in 1903 by Steindorff[9] and the rosettes on the gilt copper bands used to tighten the coffin and found in the Sixth Dynasty mastaba of Kaemsenu.[10] The princess' fillet is massive (plate 5), with a central rosette which measures seven centimetres across, and the horizontal axis of the pairs of papyrus blooms is more than eight centimetres, contrasting sharply with the princess' delicate gold necklace (plate 6). The fifty figures on the necklace rather like dandelion buds are, according to Keimer, meant to represent the beetle, *Agrypnus notodonta*, dedicated to the goddess Neith and the forerunner of the scarab which was to become so fashionable.[11] These little golden beetles have loops fixed to their heads, through which a gold wire passes. A second wire is threaded through holes in the centre of their bodies, so that the whole necklace is held together fairly firmly. The particularly charming effect of this necklace results from the plain treatment of a single, fairly simple motif in a precious material.

The Gīza burial ground yielded up a few more necklaces of the Fourth Dynasty period. Most of them consist of free-hanging strings of beads of various materials — gold, semi-precious stones and faience — with a single semicircular fastening. In some of the necklaces there are spacers, formed by metal plaques with holes for the strings to pass through, either oblong or zigzag, perhaps formed on the hieroglyph *n*. It is surprising that not a single example of a broad collar necklace like that of princess Nofret was found here, although it was certainly popular and often worn. Beads, gold spacers and fastenings found in the unknown princess' tomb were reconstructed as armlets and anklets, which are also common items in the jewellery of women up to the end of the Middle Kingdom.[12]

From the Fifth Dynasty onwards, men, as well as women, wore broad collar necklaces which, judging by contemporary reliefs, appear to have been of two common types. One has multiple rows of closely strung cylindrical beads, usually indicated on reliefs by parallel lines or by broader bands of colour with lines of white in between, ending either in drop pendants or without further ornament. The colour schemes are blue, red and green or blue-green; black and green; green and yellow, and so on.[13] The other type consists of strings of beads with the spacers indicated in various ways. At regular intervals the strings pass through oblong or rhomboid spacers arranged in vertical lines; these spacers, sometimes single, elsewhere double or even triple, correspond to the metal spacers used in real necklaces and bracelets. On the reliefs there is only evidence of oblong or slightly rhomboid spacers.[14] The zigzag form found in Gīza is nowhere shown and may have been popular only under the Fourth Dynasty, falling into oblivion later. While the necklaces without spacers are joined together all along their length, forming a compact and immobile whole, the use of spacers made it possible to join the single strings more flexibly; the result was an openwork effect where smaller beads and greater distances between them were used. The necklaces made with spacers appear to have been definitely more popular with men, while women are more often shown with the compact collars.

A unique exception is the broad necklace consisting of rows of roundels and two rows of flower motifs painted on a limestone figure of a maidservant making beer. In view of the social position of the woman we cannot assume that the painting represents real jewels; it is more probable that the Egyptian artist painted wreaths of flowers fixed on some kind of cloth backing.[15]

Besides broad collars, women of the Fifth and Sixth Dynasties wore 'chokers', narrow bands of beads fastened closely round the throat.[16] From the way these are painted they also seem to have been made of several strings of beads fixed with downward rows of spacers. Bracelets were worn on the wrist and anklets on the ankle. The sets of bracelets reaching right up to the elbow made way for broader bracelets which seem from the reliefs to have been made in the same way as the 'chokers', with several strings of beads with spacers. Anklets are portrayed in the same fashion. The popularity of these bracelets lasted throughout the Old Kingdom, the Middle and even into the New Kingdom.

Few examples of the *wesekh* type of broad collar necklaces have survived from the time of the Old Kingdom. The most beautiful is the one from Impy's tomb, consisting of double rows of greenish cylindrical beads and single rows of tiny gold beads.[17] The gold fastenings are semicircular, and the collar ends in a row of gold pendants which Keimer believes to be an unidentified beetle.[18] However, in ornamental borders lotus buds are stylized in exactly the same way, and where there is nothing to suggest the colour, it is difficult to determine from the shape alone whether a beetle or a lotus bud is meant.

High-born Egyptians of the Sixth Dynasty often wore fillets. Unlike women's fillets, inspired by wreaths of natural flowers combining elements of a wreath with a ribbon, the original men's fillets were tied at the nape of the neck so as to bring the bows forward towards the ears and leave the ends hanging down the back. In the Fifth Dynasty, this head ornament was the prerogative of the king, and included the uraeus serpent, symbol of royalty, its body twisted round the fillet. When, later, royal power waned, the lesser nobility also assumed the right to wear fillets. Already under the Fifth Dynasty, the knot at the nape of the neck had become a clasp with a roundel in the centre and pairs of papyrus blooms on each side; this did not change until late in the dynastic era. The ribbon itself, and the loose ends, usually bore a design of alternate broad and narrow rectangles. It is interesting to note that local nobles are usually shown wearing fillets when out hunting among the papyrus reeds. This would imply that they were real woven ribbons with the practical function of holding the carefully arranged locks of their wigs in place and keeping them tidy. The clasp with a design of papyrus blossom was made by a jeweller.[19]

The rare find, so far the only one, of a gold belt in the tomb of prince Ptahshepses has recently turned the attention of scholars to this type of goldsmiths' work *(plate 8)*.[20] The basis is beaten gold with semicircular fastenings and a slightly rhomboid clasp of gold set with semi-precious stones. The surface is finely granulated with tiny beads of gold and stones strung on gold wire to form a geometrical design of diamonds and zigzags. This motif appears on the ivory bracelets of the protodynastic era, and particularly on king Narmer's belt as depicted on his famous palette. There is a similar belt engraved on an ivory statue of king Menkaurē (Mycerinus),[21] and the combination of diamond and zigzag patterns is seen on royal belts in mural paintings and reliefs up to the late dynastic period. In this connection note should be made, too, of the traces of colour on the belts of king Menkaurē in the triad groups. The pattern uses alternate broad and narrow strips in green and black,[22] one of the most common patterns often found on royal belts, the original of which was, presumably, a belt of jewellers' work, perhaps made in the same way as that of prince Ptahshepses.

In addition to jewels whose primary function was the adornment of their owner, although some of them may also have been regarded as magical amulets, there are true amulets known from the Old Kingdom. Contemporary sources show that they were worn exclusively by men and in occasional instances in great numbers. From the time of the earliest known representation of an amulet from the protodynastic era, mentioned above, they were worn on a string or chain around the neck throughout thousands of years of Egyptian culture. Sometimes, as on the stele (an upright slab with designs and inscriptions) of the lady Ihat, or the reliefs in Thiy's tomb,[23] the amulet proper is accompanied by pairs of cylinders, or pairs of long olive-shaped beads. They are often worn with *wesekh* collars. The form of the amulet is sometimes so clear that there can be no doubt about its purpose, the *ankh* hieroglyph, for example, on the reliefs of Khabausokar, or the *ib* hieroglyph in the reliefs in Thiy's tomb and that of Usernetjer.[24] But elsewhere it is very difficult to determine its significance. However, as special studies have been made of Egyptian amulets, only their artistic treatment needs to be considered in this book.

IV

THE MIDDLE KINGDOM

Under the Middle Kingdom, jewellery reached aesthetic heights and a unity of style rarely met with in this field. The previous era, beginning with the late Sixth Dynasty, had already shown signs of the direction in which jewellery would develop. Again much of our knowledge is based on contemporary illustration, particularly from the rock tombs of Upper Egypt, as well as on the few rare examples which have survived.

The types of fillet do not change in the transitional period, but the form of a ribbon knotted at the nape of the neck and decorated with a clasp of two papyrus blooms, worn also by women, is more prevalent. It is an interesting point that in scenes where the monarch is accompanied by his wife, wearing her fillet, he is almost without exception shown in a wig only, without a fillet. High-born Egyptians continue to wear the ornamental fillet when hunting among papyrus reeds. Information about ribbon fillets is supplemented by illustrations of scenes in jewellers' workshops.[1]

The silver royal fillet belonging to king Inyotef, one of a line of rulers of that name during the Eleventh Dynasty, has been in the Leiden Museum Egyptological collection since 1828.[2] The band of silver is divided into broad and narrow sections by three and four vertical grooves; at the back it is held by a clasp with two papyrus blooms from which the shorter ends of the formalized ribbon rise slanting towards the temples while the longer ends fall over the shoulders. This rare treasure indicates that the reliefs and murals give a true impression of the object itself. Since this is a royal fillet, a golden uraeus is fixed to the front of it. The broader sections are ornamented with drop pendants set with a coloured vitreous substance and suspended by means of strings of beads fixed to the sides of the fillet. This part of the decoration appears to be of a later date than the fillet itself.

The necklaces shown in murals are mostly the popular types: *wesekh* collars of many concentric circles, with semicircular fastenings and drop pendants; or a simpler form without pendants. Among the necklaces in the scene of the jewellers' workshop on the wall of Isi's tomb in Deir el-Gebrāwi, there is a deep collar of beads with spacers and a fastening shaped like a hawk's head, a favourite design under the Twelfth Dynasty.[3] A feature of these necklaces was the counterpoise *(menkhet)* at the nape of the neck, which helped to keep the necklace in place. These counterpoises are usually shaped like slender calyces decorated with horizontal bands corresponding to the rows of beads in the collar, and end in drop pendants. Pear-shaped and oblong examples are rarer.

In some of the jewellers' workshop scenes there are necklaces reminiscent of the shape of the hieroglyph *sa*, meaning 'protection'. The broad ribbon, decorated with the usual sections, ends in front in a rhomboid plaque with drop pendants.[4] A later version, in which the plaque already resembles a proper pectoral, is used on the necklaces of the daughters of Thutihotpe in the well-known relief from el-Bersha.[5] It is a debatable point whether study of this type of plaque would produce enough evidence of its development for us to be able to consider it the forerunner of the great royal pectorals of the Twelfth Dynasty period. A related form is seen in the pectorals shaped like the symbol of the goddess Hathor with her head resting between the ends of the broad ribbon and the rhomboid plaque.[6].

From the late Sixth Dynasty onwards men, as well as women, commonly wore bracelets. From the way they are portrayed they appear to be made of several rows of small beads threaded through spacers, and in rare cases bracelets are apparently set with semi-precious stones. It is not unlikely that bands of gold or silver, decorated in the usual oblong patterns, were also used. Anklets, made in the same way as the bracelets, were worn only by women. 'Chokers' went out of fashion during the Sixth Dynasty.

Ornamental belts, most of them decorated with the usual oblong sections,[7] occasionally appear in the scenes of jewellers' workshops. The clasp in front is usually shaped like a knot with an interesting additional motif suggesting the archaic type of man's apron and decorated with drop pendants.

Fortunately our knowledge of the jeweller's art in the Middle Kingdom is not limited to what appears on tombs and coffins. Thanks to a number of fortunate discoveries the original material now in museums, particularly in Cairo and New York, is so extensive that we can consider the illustrations as supplementary sources.

In the tombs of the late Eleventh and early Twelfth Dynasties, where they have not been disturbed before their excavation, two kinds of jewellery are commonly found: those which belonged to the dead man in his lifetime and which he really wore; and those which were made for the specific purpose of adorning the dead man in his tomb, or rather, on his journey to the next world. The American Egyptologist, W. C. Hayes, thinks that this 'funerary jewellery' is deliberately old-fashioned in form.[8] It is certainly closer to the murals in the Sixth Dynasty tombs and those of the first transition period, than to that actually worn at the time. *Wesekh* collars, for instance, are frequently found in tombs, while what was actually worn includes new types of necklaces. There are also differences in the execution; whereas real jewellery is made of strong material and provided with metal spacers and fastenings, or strong strings for fastening, funerary jewellery is often of fragile faience; plaster covered with gold leaf, or gilt wood, takes the place of solid gold; the strings are weak, or absent altogether. Compared with the originals found in tombs, the pieces of jewellery depicted in contemporary murals and on coffins are mostly well-worn archaic types. The artists seem to have been primarily concerned with clear representation, and the traditional forms were undoubtedly the most suitable for the purpose. Work, such as the magnificent pieces now in the collections of Middle Kingdom jewellery, does not appear at all in the paintings of the time.

Fundamentally the types of jewellery popular under the Middle Kingdom dynasties were the same as in the previous period: necklaces, fillets, bracelets, anklets and belts. Rings are a new element and the number of the individual types and their variants within the several categories is much greater than in the previous age.

The necklace in its simplest form is a string of beads. The tombs of the late Eleventh Dynasty, most of the material from which is today in the collections of the Metropolitan Museum, New York, revealed a great many of the most varied material and execution. Contemporary paintings of everyday scenes, however, show single strings of beads, although they are somewhat more frequently painted on coffins.[9] The materials include faience, semi-precious and other coloured stones, gold and silver. The necklace belonging to queen Nefru, the wife of king Mentuhotpe, for instance, comprises small cylindrical beads of bright blue faience with a central group of twenty-seven large semi-precious stones of various shapes and colours.[10] The necklace on the well-known sarcophagus of queen Kawit, also of late in the Eleventh Dynasty, seems to have been of a similar type. She is wearing three strings of beads, two apparently made of disks and the third with seven large irregular beads in the centre. In my view the similarity is only in the arrangement of the beads. Little princess Miyet had several necklaces with her in the tomb, including a string of large, hollow, spherical, gold beads, a string of cornelians and an unusual necklace of gold rings so closely threaded on a leather string that they formed a mobile tube of gold.[11] Large spherical beads of gold or silver, made by soldering together two halves with tiny tubes at the holes for string, were new in the late Eleventh Dynasty. A string of silver beads of this type was found in the tomb of the steward Wah,[12] and they are painted on the sides of some coffins of the period. When necklaces are made of large beads of precious material, there is a preference, on the whole, for beads of identical material and shape. Of the semi-precious stones used for beads the favourites were cornelians and garnet and, above all, amethyst which, in view of its colour, is not usually combined with other stones. Many amethyst necklaces were found in Eleventh and Twelfth Dynasty tombs, including some beautiful ones of large, fine-coloured stones. Strings of small beads, however, are often made of different materials and have pendants. These are often gold shells, or well-known symbols to which magic powers were attributed, such as *udjat* (eye), the hieroglyph *sa* (protection), *ankh* (life) and so on. Sometimes there are several different small amulets on a single necklace *(plate 21c)*.

De Morgan's discovery, in 1894—5, of the tombs of the Twelfth Dynasty princesses round the pyramid of Amenemhet (Ammenemes) II in Dahshūr, and Brunton's somewhat later discovery of the tomb of another princess not far from the pyramid of Senwosret (Sesostris) II in el-Lāhūn (1913—14) revealed the jeweller's art of the Middle Kingdom in all its glory. Together with the rich funeral furniture of the tomb of Senebtisi dating from the early Twelfth Dynasty, found in 1906—7, not far from the pyramid of Amenemhet I at el-Lisht, the objects found are the pride of the Cairo Museum and the Metropolitan Museum of New York. All the items concerned have been described in detail in other publications and in catalogues so only the most outstanding need to be mentioned here.[13] It should be remembered in this connection, however, that not all the jewels were discovered in their original position. This is the case particularly with the necklaces of beads and pendants, and the bracelets. The strings on which they were threaded had disappeared and so the reconstruction of these jewels is that of today.

Of the jewellery with which the princesses were provided for the next world and which (with some exceptions) they undoubtedly wore when alive, the fillets (or diadems) are the most important. The two belonging to princess Khnumet and that of princess Sithathoriunet are the most perfect treatment of this form ever created by a master jeweller. The basic decorative motif of princess Khnumet's first fillet *(plate 12)* already appears in princess Nofret's fillet of the Fourth Dynasty: a rosette framed by two formal cup-shaped blooms. In princess Khnumet's fillet the motif is further enriched with a third bloom growing straight upwards. Here too the link in the design is formed by single rosettes, joined to the lyre-shaped blooms by means of four pointed blooms recalling a simplified lotus bloom or a cornflower petal. These little flowers finish off the upright blooms too, but the latter also differ in the way they are inlaid. Unlike the fillet of princess Nofret, the whole in this case is in openwork. The centre of the fillet, above the princess' brow, and with it the high social standing of the woman who wore it, is emphasized by a gold vulture, its wings spread between the flower blooms. A cloisonné technique was used for the incrustation; flat semi-precious stones, cut to the required shape, are fixed with a special cement in compartments formed by strips of gold soldered on to a gold foundation. The red of cornelian and the light blue-green of turquoise predominate in the colour scheme. The smaller elements in the design, like the wedge-shaped spaces between the petals of the rosettes, are inlaid with lapis lazuli.

The second fillet of princess Khnumet *(plate 13)* is remarkable for the delicate work and the original design of a subtly stylized wreath of flowers. The clasps holding a mesh of gold wire are rosettes with round cornelian centres and four papyrus blooms inlaid with turquoise. Its prototype was undoubtedly the clasp used from the Fifth Dynasty onwards to hold the ribbon fillet on the nape of the neck, which became an element in decoration as early as the Fourth Dynasty, as, for instance, on the fillet of the unknown princess from Gīza *(plate 5)*. The mesh of gold wire is also used on the fillet of Senebtisi, although the work is much simpler. Three rows of gold wire loops are linked above the brow by a single shape, a kind of double bow in twisted gold wire. It is completed by small rosettes in gold, which were attached to the wig.[14]

Unlike the unconventional girl's fillets worn by princess Khnumet, princess Sithathoriunet's is rather more of an official royal jewelled emblem *(plate 14)*. The general treatment is not unlike that of the fillets belonging to princess Nofret and the unknown princess from Gīza, for this one, too, is a band of gold adorned with stylized flower motifs. The four-petalled rosettes are related to the central rosette on the Gīza fillet. Later these rosettes were usually composed of lotus blooms, becoming a common motif in Egyptian ornament. Above the brow is an uraeus treated in a typically formalized way. Both the rosettes and the uraeus are inlaid with semi-precious stones. At the back of the fillet is an upright divided feather cut from gold leaf, and three similar double feathers hang down from both the sides and the back. The double feather at the back of the head, held in place by a simple ribbon fillet, is seen occasionally in mural paintings, for instance on the heads of the girl musicians in the tomb of Ukhhotpe.[15]

All three fillets just described, particularly the flower fillet of princess Khnumet, seem, at first sight, to be new and original in treatment. They are, nevertheless, composed of ornaments and motifs which can be traced as early as the Old Kingdom. It is thus apparent that the jewellery developed uninterruptedly, and that a number of the stages in the evolution of these motifs are not represented in the surviving evidence. It is very unlikely that the master craftsmen who made the fillets of the princesses Khnumet and Sithathoriunet had ever seen the painting of princess Nofret's fillet, or the diadem of the unknown princess from Gīza. Their ability to create ever new variants of ancient ornaments and motifs is amazing. The lost links in this chain will probably never be found, for there is little hope of new finds, and the jewels represented on the mural paintings do not present sufficiently detailed evidence.

Some of the mummies of princesses of the Twelfth Dynasty are adorned with *wesekh* collars and from the material used (gold, silver and semi-precious stones) it might be assumed that these collars were not merely 'funerary' jewellery such as was found in Senebtisi's tomb. The collars of princess Ita and princess Itaweret, however, end in semicircular fastenings of archaic form. Judging from the jewel-boxes of princess Sithathoriunet, princess (later queen) Mereret and princess Khnumet, laid separately in their tombs, this type of necklace was not very popular. It seems likely that in spite of the precious material used, these broad collar necklaces were made especially for the funeral furniture. On the other hand, the other necklaces found in the princesses' jewel-boxes are of a newer type not to be seen in contemporary paintings.

The linking of two separate strings of beads by vertical elements, usually larger elongated beads, had been common since the Old Kingdom.[16] The same method was sometimes used to join the tips of the pendants on the broad collars. One of the necklaces of princess Khnumet is made up of two strings of small gold beads linked by a series of symbolical motifs and completed by drop pendants. The fastenings are shaped like falcon's heads *(plate 18)*. The modern reconstruction of this necklace was based partly on the size of the pieces found singly in the tomb, and partly on the way some of the small gold beads had remained lying between the loops even after the string itself had fallen to pieces. The symmetrically arranged hieroglyphs, beginning with the centre *ankh* on the mat *hetep*, are of unusually beautiful and precise outline inlaid with cornelian, lapis lazuli, turquoise and green felspar. A similar necklace of closely threaded groups of the three hieroglyphs, *ankh*, *djed* and *was*, was certainly made up in the same way. All the pieces are provided with loops for fastening at the lower end as well. In the photograph in the catalogue of Cairo Museum (no. 53020), they are threaded on a single string of beads as free-hanging pendants.

Another piece of reconstruction work which is correct is that of the gold necklace of princess Mereret. It has round beads of semi-precious stones suspended from short grooved rods by strips of gold. The archaeologist who discovered the treasure first threaded these pendants on a string of large amethyst beads found in the same place, and added a different pendant in the centre. This combination of large amethyst beads with the pendants of cornelian, lapis lazuli and turquoise clashes, however, with the refined taste of the Twelfth Dynasty. A new reconstruction using small gold beads and an inlaid fastening found on the same spot has resulted in a wonderful jewel whose noble simplicity can compare with the finest works of modern craftsmanship *(plate 19)*. Among the jewels of princess Khnumet are some gold pendants on chains which are usually considered, on account of the granulated work and the use of some un-Egyptian motifs, to be at least in part imports from Crete *(plates 17c and 17d)*. There is perhaps evidence of the use of granulation in the Aegean cultural sphere earlier than in Egypt. This technique is used for some of the motifs which are undeniably Egyptian, however, like the five-pointed star pendants resembling those on the princess' fillet. It would seem more probable, therefore, that these jewels were the work either of a Cretan craftsman working at the Egyptian court, or an Egyptian who had learned the granulation technique from a Cretan jeweller.

The royal pectorals form a distinct group. Their earliest origin must be sought in the simple amulets known from predynastic times, and like the amulets, pectorals were also credited with the power of protecting their wearers. In the amulets this power was attributed to a single symbol (an animal, bird, beetle and so on), while the pectorals had a large number of protective symbols related to one particular individual who, in all the pectorals of the Twelfth Dynasty, is the monarch, whose first name in a cartouche forms the centre of the design. This design forms a rebus which can be expressed in a brief slogan. On the pectoral of Amenemhet III, for example *(plate 11)*, appears 'May Rē Harakhty give life for millions of years to Nemarē'; or it may be more involved, such as on the pectoral of Senwosret III *(plate 9)*: 'May the goddess Nekhbet protect Khakaurē, who conquers his enemies like the sun god.'

The way these pectorals developed cannot as yet be reliably deduced, for a number of stages are missing. One special type of necklace formed, when viewed from above, a unit representing the hieroglyph *sa*, the symbol of protection, particularly the second variant of the character. On the painting of Thutihotpe's daughters at el-Bersha this rhomboid pendant has a number of drop pendants hanging from it, while the centre of the design is taken up by a symbolic sun-disk between two uraei and Lower Egyptian crowns.[17] The jewel painted here must have been in openwork and set with semi-precious stones. It would appear that the symbolic motif, which was a later addition to the pendant, in the course of time acquired the predominant significance. It was then treated as an independent unit, apart from the original composition of the whole necklace. This is mere hypothesis; there is still too much wanting for any certainty.

The pectorals of the Middle Kingdom are of two kinds. The more frequent is the 'enclosed' form which has an architectural framework resembling the façade of the type of light pavilions used on such occasions as celebrations of the king's anniversary (the *sed* festival). The ornamental motifs used in the surround are often inspired by architectural forms; cornices and slender pillars in the form of stems topped by lotus blooms. In plate 9 the strictly architectural treatment is forgotten, for the stem divides and one bloom leans over, forming part of the central composition. In most cases both the base and the vertical elements in the surround are decorated with alternating broad and narrow rectangles *(plates 9* and *10).* The 'open' form of pectoral is rarer. Here the symbolic design is not framed by a surround; in some cases the base is formed by a narrow horizontal moulding *(plate 11),* elsewhere this remnant of the original surround has disappeared, as, for instance, in the incomplete pectoral ornamented with a winged scarab found in Riqqa.[18] Both forms continued to develop, but the 'enclosed' form remained more conservative.

As in the pectoral of Amenemhet III *(plate 10)* the motto is arranged almost symmetrically with only slight deviations necessitated by the hieroglyphs. The pectorals of the Twelfth Dynasty are strongly reminiscent of the involved heraldic compositions of the later Middle Ages. They differ, however, in the greater significance given to each separate element and in the fact that they are bound up with the person of the ruler, while the mediaeval coats of arms are primarily the symbol of a whole line.

All the royal pectorals of the Middle Kingdom are in openwork with cloisonné incrustation in the usual semi-precious stones, in some cases perhaps replaced by coloured vitreous substances. The gold reverse is as carefully finished as the obverse, the details being engraved and chased.

Menat necklaces have a special place in the history of Egyptian jewellery. They are composed of a large number of free hanging strings of beads, both ends of which are caught in a small cup from which single strings of variously shaped beads hang down the back. During the Middle Kingdom they ended in two long drop pendants, which as time went on, increased in size until they were replaced by a single counterpoise. These are flat, elongated rhombs ending in a round or oval plaque decorated with rosettes. These counterpoises, which acquired the name of the whole necklace, served, or were meant to serve, the same purpose as those on *wesekh* necklaces. G. Möller suggested that they also acted as amulets protecting their wearer from behind.[19] This is given as the explanation of why they later acquired the form of the goddess Hathor. In contemporary paintings, *menat* necklaces are more often held in the hand than worn, and once the counterpoise became more elaborate women carried them only in their hands. In so far as they were used as necklaces at all, they adorned men rather than women. There are three priests of the goddess Hathor painted on the wall of tomb 60 in Thebes, wearing *menat* necklaces round their necks and carrying castanets.[20] In Senbi's tomb in Meir, dating from the early Twelfth Dynasty, there are again three priests of the same goddess and three priestesses wearing *menat* necklaces, the priestesses holding sistrums.[13] Another piece of evidence dating from the later Middle Kingdom is the well-known statue in Cairo Museum of Amenemhet III in priestly garb, from Mit-Fara. Besides other priestly attributes, the king is wearing a *menat* on his shoulders.

Besides the strings of large and small beads and their pendants, about which there is no doubt how they were worn, the princesses' tombs in Dashūr and el-Lāhūn also yielded large hollow gold beads shaped like cowrie shells or like two-headed leopards, the purpose of which is not clear. Originally it was thought that they were parts of a necklace, but now scholars suggest that they belonged to ornamental belts.[22] Some belts have actually been found; one belonging to Hapy has eight cowrie shell beads linked by several rows of beads of lapis lazuli[23] and a different type belonging to Senebtisi. Similar belts are painted on wooden and faience female figures found in tombs of the Middle Kingdom and of the following period of the Hyksos kings. C. Desroches Noblecourt has devoted an extensive study to the significance of these figures and believes that they embody womanhood, that they are symbolic concubines for the dead man in the life to come, the women who maintain and revere his manly powers.[24] This would appear to be more acceptable than the older view that the belts were specifically worn by dancing girls. It is remarkable, however, that the belts are painted exclusively on these idols and never appear in contemporary scenes of home life or public occasions. Not until later, during the New Kingdom, do naked girls wear these belts; they are either very young, or obviously lowly music girls, dancing girls and servants. This had led to the assumption that women's jewelled belts were not originally meant to be worn in public, but only for the intimate life of the harem. The fact that they were placed round the dead woman's hips may also have had a sexual significance.

Other iconographical evidence, however, suggests that the large cowrie shells were also sometimes used in necklaces. Queen Kawit at her morning toilet, depicted on her sarcophagus, has a necklace round her neck with seven unusually large beads, elongated and irregular in shape, which look as if they might be cowrie shells. A group of seven beads occupies the centre of the necklace, the rest being apparently smaller beads. Since the arrangement is similar to that in queen Nofru's necklace, discussed earlier, it might be worth trying to reconstruct some of the existing groups of gold cowrie shell beads in this way.

The bracelets found in the princesses' graves and those of private individuals of the Twelfth Dynasty are both of metal and of beads. The metal bracelets are for the most part simple bands of gold, flattened in cross-section, and sometimes ornamented on the obverse with shallow horizontal grooves.[26] Bead bracelets are either of single strings, sometimes with the addition of two recumbent golden lions *(plate 21b)*, or of broad bands of many strings of beads connected by spacers and fastened by special fasteners either sliding or jointed, with a moveable pin. The bead bracelets were often found scattered and have had to be put together again from separate pieces, for museum purposes. The guide to such reconstructions is either a bracelet found in a better state of repair, or contemporary illustrations.[27]

In the period of the Middle Kindom, the existing range of jewels in Egypt was widened by the addition of a new element, rings. It has been assumed that these were imported from Crete, since two rings with granulated decoration, belonging to princess Mereret, seem, both in style and in technique, to belong to the Aegean cultural orbit.[28] On the other hand, a second type of ring found in this period bears all the signs of native tradition, and its functional simplicity does not point to the use of more advanced Cretan rings as a model. The Egyptian ring-type may have developed from the cylindrical and button seals and the scarab seals worn on a string round the neck. In the rings, the string is replaced by a piece of gold wire drawn lengthwise through the body of the insect and tied in a knot with the two ends simply turned backwards *(plate 16)*. Since a knot of wire on the inside of the finger was probably very uncomfortable, a new way of fastening the scarab on was soon found: both the ends of the wire were passed through the body of the scarab and turned alongside it, so that the inner surface of the ring was smooth *(plate 71c)*. Later on the thin wire was replaced by thicker wire, the ends of which were flattened and bored to allow a separate piece of wire, passing through the body of the scarab, to be fixed to it *(plate 71d)*. The scarabs themselves, turning on a pin and inscribed on the under side with hieroglyphs or decorations, were made of various materials. Of the semi-precious stones, the favourites were lapis lazuli, whose deep blue colour resembled the sacred beetle, and some other semi-precious and coloured stones, mostly green ones, as well as glazed steatite and faience. Some of the most beautiful rings are the scarabs belonging to princess Mereret and Sithathoriunet, set with cornelian, lapis lazuli and turquoise *(plate 16)*. Apart from the Cretan imports found in the tomb of princess Mereret, these scarab rings are the only type known and worn in the Middle Kingdom.

Soon after the death, in 1797 B.C., of the last important ruler of the Twelfth Dynasty, Amenemhet III, royal power began to wane, and the second intermediate period began. This era covers the ephemeral governments of the Thirteenth to Seventeenth Dynasties and includes the rule of the 'Hyksos' kings. Relics of the period are somewhat rare, for like most ages of uncertainty and chaos, it was marked by stagnation in the arts and, naturally enough, a shortage of precious materials which was certainly most felt by the jewellers. The jewellery found in the tombs of el-Asasīf (now in the Metropolitan Museum, New York) indicates that it was during this period that the first ear-rings appeared in Egypt, brought by conquerors from the East. There are two major types: hoops of gold or gilt bronze with a gap between the ends, so that they were probably fixed in the same way as the clip-on ear-rings of today; and spirals of gold or silver wire attached either in the same way, or threaded through holes in the lobes of the ear.[29] Beads for necklaces were again made of the most varied material, with the cheaper faience predominating, but semi-precious stones and gold are found, too. Every possible shape of bead was used, spherical beads of all sizes being the most popular; a new fashion was for large disk or lens-shaped beads, threaded close together, which we find still in the late dynastic era. All the common types of amulet are also found; the *udjat* eye, the scarabs, hearts, flies, shells and so on. For the most part this jewellery was not of great artistic value, and it is not easy to assign a date to the pieces found. The one considerable contribution to the development of the jeweller's art, particularly in the time of the Eighteenth Dynasty, were the ear-rings, which brought the possibility of new designs.

V

THE NEW KINGDOM

The most valuable pieces of jewellery of the New Kingdom to have survived belong largely to the important discovery of the tombs of queen Ahhotpe, of the princesses of the harem of Thutmose (Tuthmosis) III and of Tutankhamūn, which were either untouched or slightly damaged; robbers had managed to get in, but not carry their booty away. All three were the tombs of kings or their families and represent the highest in the jeweller's art of the day, providing us with an outline of its development from the beginning to the end of the Eighteenth Dynasty. Comparing what has survived with what is depicted in murals and reliefs, it is clear that only a part of what was produced in the jewellers' workshops has come down to us. Jewellery adorned not only human beings but the statues of the gods, and certainly formed part of the temple treasures, but the rich crowns which adorned heads of kings and gods in the New Kingdom have not survived. Nevertheless, the few existing treasures of the royal court are sufficient evidence of the golden magnificence in which the great of that day lived.

The first of these three great finds is the treasure of queen Ahhotpe, mother of the founder of the Eighteenth Dynasty, king Ahmose (Amosis), discovered in 1859 by the famous French Egyptologist, Mariette. This wonderful collection of jewels and ornamental jewelled weapons shows that the period of the Hyksos kings did not affect the art of the jeweller in Egypt. Tradition lived on, and if the jewels of queen Ahhotpe are compared with those of the princesses of the Twelfth Dynasty, it seems incredible that they are separated by nearly three centuries, two-thirds of which were torn by strife and uncertainty. However, the value of the material itself and the skill and craftsmanship that go into the making of each piece a unique work of art means that jewellery is less susceptible to changes of taste and fashion than, say, dress. Even so, the continuity of tradition in Egyptian jewellery is remarkable; it shows fewer breaks with the distant past than monumental art does.

Closer examination of the treasure of queen Ahhotpe does reveal certain changes, albeit within strictly traditional lines. There are one or two pieces in the collection that derive directly from the art of the Middle Kingdom as though there had been no interval. This applies primarily to the pectoral of king Ahmose *(plate 22)* and a pair of bracelets with many rows of small beads of gold and semi-precious stones *(plate 27)*. A certain change in taste can nevertheless be seen in two bracelets made in separate sections joined by a hinge and a pin. The first bears the figure of the vulture goddess Nekhbet with spread wings *(plate 28)* while the other has a chased ornament in gold set in lapis lazuli.[1] There are new trends in the treatment of the traditional *wesekh* collar necklaces. The way the queen's collar has been reconstructed for display in the Cairo Museum *(plate 24)* is not absolutely reliable, as it would probably be difficult to wear it in real life like this; nevertheless, it does show in its individual elements the difference between the new approach and tradition. The rows of beads are no longer set close together and held firm, and the stereotyped cylindrical beads of various colours have been replaced by a large number of gold ornamental pieces, some geometrical, others with plant and animal motifs, threaded on single strings or perhaps on gold wire. The queen's breast was no longer hidden beneath a flat bead shield, but glittered with a gold lace collar which has something in common with princess Khnumet's necklaces, also made up of single pieces freely arranged between two strings of beads; but the lively colours and the gleaming metal of these necklaces are quite different in effect from the striking single tone of the gold.

Single pendants on gold chains also came into fashion, the best known being undoubtedly the one with three gold flies *(plate 23)*; the large scarab inlaid with lapis lazuli is less well known.[2] It is impossible to tell, of course, which of the jewels were really worn by queen Ahhotpe and which were the property of her son, Ahmose. From older finds and from paintings, it appears that single amulets were only worn by men. Several small amulets worn as pendants are more common for women, and they also wore a single cornelian bead known as a *seweret*, which was probably also a protective charm. Whether the *seweret* was simply a part of the funeral furniture or an adornment worn in real life is unclear.[3]

Among the new types of bracelets are large gold bangles of square cross-section, with bows of gold wire on the corners *(plate 26)*, and bracelets with curved, barrel-shaped walls, favoured by men of the Eighteenth Dynasty.[4] It is curious that there is not a single pair of ear-rings in the whole collection, although they seem to have been included in the furniture of private tombs for some time previously.

Weapons with jewelled handles had, undoubtedly, a tradition of long standing. A dagger with an inlaid handle is a Twelfth Dynasty example from the tomb of princess Ita at Dahshūr. In her funeral furniture queen Ahhotpe had both ornamental daggers and axes which, made of precious materials, represent an archaic type known from the predynastic era. It is interesting to see how, in the course of time, a sense of fitness for use is expressed in the treatment of this instrument; the gentle curve of the handle, with its elegant widening, heralds the efforts of modern designers to find the most functional form for everyday tools. The handle of king Ahmose's ceremonial axe is indeed shaped to fit the human hand, and curved so as to give the most effective blow with the minimum of effort *(plate 29)*. The handles of other common tools of Eighteenth Dynasty Egypt show similar functional beauty.

A magnificent representation of life at the royal court, of the religious and other ceremonies connected with it, and of the great events that marked the reign of queen Makarē Hatshepsut is to be found in the reliefs in her tomb temple in Deir el-Bahari. They also form a fashion parade of both dress and jewellery. It is, of course, an open question how far the evidence of contemporary iconography is to be trusted as a record of fact. The treasures of the Twelfth Dynasty princesses show that not everything that was actually worn was portrayed by the artists, who tended to be conservative and to treat jewels often as symbols rather than as something they saw being worn. And the reliefs in Deir el-Bahari must be considered in this light also. Both gods and goddesses, and kings and queens, are shown wearing *wesekh* collars with drop pendants of the conventional type. An exception is Thutmose (Tuthmosis) III, who is shown wearing an open pectoral with the hieroglyph *ib* (heart) in the centre, flanked by two uraei bearing the disk of the sun on their heads.[5] A third sun is placed above the hieroglyph *ib*. Another interesting detail is the way a *menat* necklace is depicted round the neck of the sacred cow of the goddess Hathor, with a counterpoise ending in a rosette, lying on the animal's back.[6] On another occasion the sacred cow is shown wearing round its neck the symbol of the goddess, seen on necklaces in the early Middle Kingdom period.[7]

Men wear bracelets on their wrists, while goddesses and women have both bracelets and anklets, which later went quite out of fashion. Both are shown here in the usual form. The broader central band is usually ornamented with a rectangular pattern, sometimes double, which is probably meant to be a stylized representation of bead bracelets with spacers, but it is so schematically treated that it gives no idea of the actual details of the work. There is a similar ornament on the king's belts, while in rarer cases a diamond and zigzag motif is used, as on the belt of prince Ptahshepses of the Fifth Dynasty. Only the little princess Khebitnofru is shown naked, with a belt round her hips, two strings of beads over a broad collar necklace, bracelets on her wrists and anklets on her feet. On her head is a fillet seen in profile, apparently consisting of six circular roundels with rosettes, increasing in size from the brow towards the nape of the neck; an uraeus is fixed in the centre between them.[8] The queens are mostly wearing strange 'vulture head-dresses'. These, which seem to have been, at least partly, made by jewellers, take the form of the vulture of the goddess Mut, the bird's head rising above the brow of the wearer and the wings falling down on either side of her head. The tail, spread like a starched and pleated flare, adorns the back of her head. No original example of this head-dress has survived.

With few exceptions, then, we find in these reliefs at Deir el-Bahari the same range of jewellery as on the walls of Middle Kingdom tombs. For the most part they are traditional elements. However, the artist has made an interesting distinction between typically Egyptian jewellery and that worn by the queen of the land of Punt and her court.[9] This fat queen is wearing a necklace with three large round plaques strung on three strings. Her companion wears a similar necklace, on a smaller scale, while the men carrying gifts have round or oval amulets on thick strings round their necks. The queen's bracelets and anklets are of double strings or bands, their design unbroken. However, the ribbon fillets tied at the nape of the neck are depicted in the typical Egyptian manner. Egyptian artists always did their best to show the exact difference between native and foreign ornament. However, the question remains whether the way the foreign patterns and the foreign jewellery is represented here corresponds to what the artist really saw, or whether it is only the result of an effort to make clear the distinction.

The three princesses Menwi, Merti and Menhet, of the harem of Thutmose III, whose tomb in Sheikh Abd el-Qurna was discovered by thieves a little before the archaeologists got there, were either young contemporaries of queen Makarē Hatshepsut, or contemporaries of her daughter Nofrurē. Their names suggest foreign birth, perhaps Syrian, and the jewellery in their tomb is markedly different from that depicted in the Deir el-Bahari tomb. From the solidity with which they were made it can be assumed that all the jewels were worn by the princesses during their lifetime, but they have suffered considerable damage from water which seeped into the tomb, and from careless handling by the villagers of Qurna, who stole them.[10] W.C. Hayes considers this jewellery typical of the New Kingdom, with no parallels in a previous age, and attributes the over-decoration of some of the pieces to Oriental influence.[11] Yet, although there are no close parallels, detailed examination shows that this jewellery, too, has its origins purely in Egypt with few concessions to non-Egyptian taste. The craftsmanship, however, is of a much lower standard than that of the jewellery of the Twelfth Dynasty princesses or queen Ahhotpe.

The most surprising items in the funeral furniture of these princesses are the head-dresses. Some of these consist of egg-shaped gold leaf coverings for the crown of the head, and a net of vertical rows of gold rosettes inlaid with stones, suspended to cover the hair. This seems to be a development of a style which can be seen beginning in the time of the Middle Kingdom. In a similar way the hair of the mummy of Senebtisi was caught in a fillet with rows of gold rosettes fixed to the locks. The remains of gold sequins arranged in a chessboard pattern on a carved wooden head of a woman from el-Lisht looks as though they formed a complete network and were not merely scattered hair ornaments.[12] In the Metropolitan Museum, New York, the gold tubes found in the treasure of princess Sithathor at el-Lāhūn have been reconstructed to form an almost unbroken head-dress of gold strands hanging from the fillet and covering practically the whole of the wig.[13] Although, by this arrangement, the two side-pieces of the fillet are hidden and lose their decorative function, it is certainly correct to assume that the gold tubes were some form of hair ornament. The unusual jewelled head-dress of the princesses of Thutmose's harem thus had forerunners in the Middle Kingdom.

Other fillets with rosettes and pairs of gazelle heads also draw on a tradition which goes far back into the Old Kingdom. The uraeus or the vulture Nekhbet is probably replaced by gazelle heads because the princesses came from a royal harem. Not being first wives, queens, or even Egyptian princesses of the blood, they had no right to wear a royal emblem or the 'vulture head-dress'.

The tombs of the three concubines also yielded evidence of the development of various smaller items of jewellery. A new type of fastening is found on the princesses' broad collar necklaces; shaped like lotus blooms, under the New Kingdom it replaced both the semicircular and the hawk's head type.[14] Some charming bracelets with broad fastenings graced by five recumbent cats in different coloured semi-precious stones can be traced back to the bracelets with pairs of lions from the time of the Middle Kingdom *(plate 21b)*.[15] The princesses had an interesting type of broad bracelet made in two parts with decorations imitating rows of small beads with spacers of the older type.[16] The decorated belts also draw on the traditions of the Middle Kingdom, but different elements appear in the choice and treatment of new motifs and in the way they are arranged.[17] The ear-rings found in this tomb are a completely new item of jewellery, previously found only in the tombs of private persons and wrongly believed to be hair ornaments.[18] It is possible that the princesses brought this form of jewellery with them from their homeland, and it is worth noting that ear-rings are not found in scenes from aristocratic life until the time of Thutmose IV, roughly three quarters of a century later.

Unfortunately, there have been no substantial finds of jewellery from the following century, during which the New Kingdom reached the height of its prosperity after the successful campaigns of Thutmose III. For knowledge of what the ladies and the highly-placed men of the time wore in the way of accessories, the isolated items found must be supplemented by the wealth of representational information on tomb walls, in mural paintings, reliefs and statues. Here again, in spite of the innumerable varieties portrayed, contemporary artists do not give a complete record of everything that was worn and considered fashionable at the time although, in the case of some types of jewellery, they provide our only evidence. The 'vulture head-dress' described above and the complicated crowns worn by kings and gods are known only from representations.

A new type of fillet worn by women from the time of Amenhotpe II appears in paintings but it is difficult to determine whether it was necessarily the work of jewellers. The origin of these fillets would seem to have been the simple ribbon tied at the back and fixed above the brow with a lotus bloom or bud. In the tomb of Wah, of the time of Thutmose III,[19] a lady at a banquet and girl musicians amusing the company wear them. Later the fillets become more ornamental, with rows of lotus petals fixed to them. A bull in Thenro's tomb, dating from the time of Amenhotpe II, has a collar of lotus petals and a simpler but similar ribbon round its horns.[20] From the time of Amenhotpe II various more or less complicated types of fillets, some with a lotus above the forehead, appear to be common as exclusively feminine ornaments. Most of them do not reach right to the nape of the neck, which is left free, but in some cases the ends of the ribbon are shown tied together. The colour schemes are predominantly pale green, pale blue and white, with a certain amount of red in some cases. This suggests that the fillets may have been made of fresh flowers, most likely of lotus blooms. It is not impossible, however, that some were made of durable materials and that the imitation petals were of faience, semi-precious stones and some sort of vitreous material. During this period men ceased wearing fillets and wear no head ornament even in hunting scenes.

Both men and women still wear *wesekh* collars. The murals show a great many variations both in the arrangement of the rows and in the shape of the component parts. Gold and semi-precious stones are used, as well as the cheaper glass and faience. An example of a complex broad collar is the faience *wesekh* found in el-Amārna: the first row is of cornflowers, the second poppy petals, the third small bunches of grapes, the fourth of alternate white and cornflower petals, the fifth dates, and the sixth and last is of white lotus petals with blue tips. Other combinations make use of palm leaves and the fruit of the mandrake.[21] In the gold collar worn by Amenhotpe IV, the first row is of small plaques inlaid with a bow pattern and linked by elongated tube-shaped beads; gold vases and dates make up the rest and the fastenings are shaped like lotus blooms.[22]

By this time *menat* necklaces were exclusively carried only by women, although they are occasionally seen worn by gods. The counterpoise are elongated and rhomboid in shape, ending in a slightly oval plaque with a rosette; later their place was sometimes taken by stylized figures representing the head of the goddess Hathor. It has been thought that, from the beginning, these necklaces were symbols of fertility and were generally linked with the idea of birth and rebirth.[23]

For men, particularly from the time of Amenhotpe III, a new type of necklace made of two or more rows of large flat lens-shaped beads became fashionable. The first known examples are found in the much older tombs of the Hyksos period. Amenhotpe III himself wears one on a relief in the tomb of Khaemhet in Thebes, and so does the steward of the royal stables, Thay, in a statue now in the Cairo Museum. The 'god's father' Ay is literally wreathed in these necklaces in the well-known rewards scene in el-Amārna.[24] Sometimes the lens-shaped beads form the first two or three rows in a broad collar, and they may also have been worn over one. The necklace (or bracelet?) shown in plate 52 is of red and yellow gold and blue faience, found in the tomb of Tutankhamūn.

It is an interesting point that the paintings of the time hardly ever show pectorals, although the large collection found in Tutankhamūn's tomb shows that they never went out of fashion. There is a pectoral shaped like a winged scarab with the disk of the sun on its head and the hieroglyph *shenu* under its back legs in a scene of a jeweller's workshop in the tomb of Nebamūn and Ipuky, from the reign of Amenhotpe III.[25] Besides this form, which remained popular until late in the dynastic era, another, with the motif of an open lotus bloom and two buds hanging on a broad double string with the typical alternating broad and narrow strips, also appears on the tomb. This motif was more often used for fastenings than as a separate pectoral.

During this period, bracelets, like necklaces, were worn by both men and women on their wrists and arms. Women favoured the traditional type with alternate narrow and broad strips of ornament made either of strings of beads with spacers, or of solid gold with incrustation ornament, like those of the princesses from the harem of Thutmose III. Men wore this type only round their wrists; higher up their arms they wore broader double or triple bands of gold. Where the middle band is painted deep blue it was presumably inlaid with lapis lazuli or blue glass. Occasionally men are shown wearing round their wrists barrel-shaped bracelets known from queen Ahhotpe's treasure; the central boss of these is sometimes painted blue. Both types, the plain gold and those with blue centres, can be seen in the painting in the tomb of Nebamūn and Ipuky referred to above. In addition to their wrist bracelets, elegant ladies of the time wore round their forearm another pair of bands of gold inlaid with semi-precious stones, usually narrow and sometimes loose. Elsewhere the treatment and the width of both sorts of bracelets are the same. Anklets, which are a common feminine ornament in the Middle Kingdom and are still seen occasionally in the early Eighteenth Dynasty, had by now gone right out of fashion.

The ear-rings already worn by the princesses of the harem of Thutmose III begin to appear fairly frequently in murals in the rock tombs from the reign of Thutmose IV onwards. The theory advanced by Möller, that it was thanks to this monarch's queen, a princess from the kingdom of Mitanni in Asia Minor, that ear-rings became known at the Egyptian court, is thus disproved.[26] What was actually worn at the royal court was usually in advance of what was painted on the walls of tombs. The most frequent type of ear-rings found in contemporary paintings are large gold hoops, plaques with rosettes, and concentric rings. Nowhere in the paintings are there ear-rings made of several gold rings of equal size joined together as found in the tomb of the three princesses. The reason for this may be that it is not easy to draw them realistically, and that it was also difficult to find a symbol which would comply with the Egyptian desire for clarity. The other forms found in tombs of the Eighteenth Dynasty were no more popular with painters of relief carvers either, for these small ornaments could not play a significant role in the composition. For the same reason rings do not appear, although they are known to have been generally worn under the New Kingdom.

The last jewelled accessories, particularly for men, are ornamental belts. Several types can be seen in mural paintings, and it appears that in the dynastic period they were the privilege of gods and pharaohs, with the possible exception of members of the royal family. In the New Kingdom period, belts, fastened in front with an oblong or oval clasp, increased in width at the back. They were single, double or triple, decorated either with a diamond and zigzag pattern, alternate wide and narrow strips, or even with a scale pattern. Various arrangements of fringes are fixed to the clasp, usually ending in uraeus heads.

Ornamental belts for women are common in the scenes of social occasions from the time of Thutmose IV, whereas up to his reign they were rare. Slightly later than the belt of the little princess in the Deir el-Bahari relief is a scene in the tomb of Wah showing two girls playing a lyre and a double pipe, wearing transparent sleeved dresses reaching almost to their ankles, and belts made up of large plaques painted in red.[27] The belts appear to have been worn under the dresses next to the skin. At a slightly later date music and dancing girls, servants and very young girls are usually shown naked in social life, wearing only ornamental belts round their hips. These rather narrow belts, which are often double, are usually painted yellow and decorated with red, blue and sometimes green plaques. In reality they must have been made of gold, set with semi-precious stones or coloured glass or faience. One of the girls in the scene painted in the tomb of Djeserkarēseneb, in the reign of Thutmose IV, is wearing a belt of two strings of white beads decorated at wide intervals with gold ornaments which appear to represent stylized knots.[28] In none of these scenes is a belt worn by an upper-class Egyptian woman, indeed the style of dress at the time made it impossible. It is a pity that there are too few finds to throw light on the full significance of this ornament, originally worn only in private and later degraded to become part of the dress of lowly women and undeveloped girls.

The tombs of private people of the Eighteenth Dynasty reveal a great deal of material including types of jewellery not found at all, or only rarely, in contemporary art. Besides the popular lens-shaped beads, necklaces of large round faience beads were worn, and probably beads of other material as well; necklaces are made of all the shapes of bead known from earlier times. Many different kinds of pendants were strung on necklaces with beads; palmettes, bunches of grapes, cornflower blooms, flies, half-moons of gold (thought to represent circles of skin bent in half and sewn together), pomegranates, and occasionally shells, although these are rarer than they were previously. The favourite material is faience, especially shades of blue and green; but red, crimson, white and yellow are also used. Semi-precious stones are still made into beads, as are other coloured stones, glazed steatite, glass, and occasionally wood covered in gold leaf.

Another group of jewels found in private graves is formed by the amulets, often miniature figures of the gods, as well as animals, birds, fish and insects. Rarer are parts of the human body corresponding in shape to some of the familiar hieroglyphs. The most popular amulets were the heart and the *udjat* eye. As in the time of the Middle Kingdom amulets representing hieroglyphs of special significance are still worn, the most frequent was *ankh*, life; then *djed*, stability; the *was*, sceptre, dominion; *nefer*, goodness, beauty; *sa*, protection; *shenu*, universal rule, dominion; the *tit* knot, a symbol of Isis, and the hieroglyph for eternity, *heh*. Besides the protective symbols there are also half-moons, stars and the *bullae* whose significance has not yet been determined. Scarabs are extremely popular in the New Kingdom, and are often beautifully worked in semi-precious stones, glazed steatite or faience, and more rarely of gold, silver or ivory.[29]

Belts and bracelets are also made of beads, the latter often of plaited strings of small beads like the handles of modern bead evening bags. Bands of faience, mostly rectangular in cross-section, are also worn, but these are probably occasional trinkets, such as gifts to be presented on festive occasions; such fragile material would hardly have been suitable for everyday wear.

The most common type of rings are those with hinged scarabs, but cowroid rings shaped originally like cowrie shells also appear, as well as plaques and amulets such as the *udjat* eye, threaded on wire twisted on to the ring, or set in a metal frame and fixed between the ends of the ring by means of pins *(plate 71a)*. Solid rings made in single pieces are also worn and fashioned with round or oval bezels flattened and engraved, or carved in relief with a symbolical motif, or an inscription. The same treatment is applied to rings where the bezel was made separately and soldered on.[30]

Most of the ear-rings found in the private graves are in the form of an incomplete hoop fastened in the same way as modern clip ear-rings. It is possible, however, judging from the size of the holes and the deformed state of the lobes in some mummies, that even fairly heavy hoops were worn through the ears. The loops were of gold, gilt bronze, semi-precious stones, shell, bone and such materials. Another type of broad metal hoop with a wavy surface and sometimes with beads cemented in the grooves, had a point at the end which was inserted into the pierced lobe. The lovely ear-rings of alabaster and a coloured vitreous substance on plate 31 show that the holes pierced in the ears of Egyptian beauties can hardly have been small. Besides these striking types, there are all kinds of rings with larger or smaller pendants of all shapes — round beads, clusters, cups, figures, and so on.[31]

The jewellery found in private tombs, however, is but a pale reflection of the magnificence of the monarch's funeral furniture or that of the members of his family. Only twice have archaeologists succeeded in finding the tomb of an Egyptian pharaoh undamaged, or practically so. The first time was 1922, when Howard Carter in the course of the seventh and last excavation he conducted for Lord Carnarvon discovered the tomb of the young Tutankhamūn, a successor of the 'heretic' king Akhenaten, which had somehow escaped notice under the tumbledown quarters of the workers cutting a later tomb. The second such discovery, by Montet in Tanis in 1940, will be discussed later.

The way in which Tutankhamūn's tomb was discovered is well-known and has been described by Carter himself as well as by later writers and by contemporary journalists, for the discovery was the sensation of the day.[32] Suffice it to say here that robbers had been at the tomb in ancient times, and damaged some of the jewellery by careless handling, but they had not succeeded in carrying off more than a fraction of what the tomb contained. The king's pure gold coffin was untouched, and the mummy when uncovered was literally buried in jewels, while more jewellery was found in boxes and caskets. The treasure of Tutankhamūn is today in the Cairo Museum; it is the greatest collection of Egyptian royal jewels in the world, but although it was discovered more than forty years ago, no detailed catalogue based on research has yet been published and single items subsequently dealt with in publications have mostly been published in Carter's original reproductions. The coloured plates in this book naturally represent only a tiny fraction of this vast treasure, but they give the reader some idea of the jewellery in the private possession of an Egyptian king of the New Kingdom. It is hard to believe that the funeral furniture of the great predecessors of Tutankhamūn and their queens was poorer than what this young and not particularly important ruler took with him to the grave. Amenhotpe III must have been buried with fantastic magnificence.

Yet even this great collection does not contain all the jewels worn by the monarch during his lifetime. The complicated ceremonial crowns, for instance, worn on various official occasions, were not found. It is possible that they were not his private property, but belonged to the royal line and were passed on to his successor.

The only ornament on the head of the dead pharaoh was a wonderful gold diadem shaped like a ribbon tied at the back.[33] The traditional form with a clasp of two papyrus blooms fixed to a circular plaque is adhered to, but a new motif appears in the decoration: rows of circular plaques set with cornelian, with gold centres on a turquoise ground. On the brow are the royal uraeus and the gold vulture head of the goddess Nekhbet, the wavy line of the uraeus' body linking the front of the fillet with the clasp at the back. The bodies of a pair of uraei form the slanting border to the tips of the ribbon pointing forward to the temples. This kind of modification within the traditional framework of the design is seen in many of the jewels in Tutankhamūn's tomb.

There were a great many necklaces both in the coffin and in the various jewel caskets of the tomb. Many are broad *wesekh* collars of the usual type, but unlike the older examples these seem to form almost a complete circle. Besides these collars there are pectorals on chains, some of the 'enclosed' type, in which a symmetrical symbolical composition is placed inside an architectonic frame. A comparison of these pectorals with the plaques worn on the breasts of the Middle Kingdom monarch shows a decided change. The centre of the design is no longer a cartouche bearing the monarch's name, but a sacred symbol, or the figure of one of the gods; the royal cartouche has become a mere attribute, showing the owner. For the most part traditional openwork with incrustation is used, but there are some solid pectorals like the one with the figure of the goddess Nut *(plate 43)* on a gold ground covered with hieroglyphs.

Besides the more conservative 'enclosed' pectorals there are examples of the 'open' type among Tutankhamūn's treasure as well. These also draw on the traditions of the Twelfth Dynasty, but gave the craftsman more opportunity to use his own imagination in the choice of theme, in the composition, and above all in the shape. The simplest in theme and form are, of course, the pectorals which represent a single symbol; an example of this is the wonderful figure of the vulture goddess Nekhbet, inlaid mainly in lapis lazuli with tiny details in cornelian and green glass *(plate 32)*. Worthy of special attention is the chain of rectangular plaques of gold and lapis lazuli, with a pair of hawks in slightly high relief on the fastening, an integral part of the composition.

Closely related to these single motif pectorals are those in the form of a scarab, or a winged scarab. They are also an expression in art form of the king's first name: Nebkheperurē[34] *(plate 44)*. The winged scarab is the central motif in several complex designs formed by a group of several symbols *(plate 48)*. The richest is undoubtedly the triangular pectoral with a scarab in chalcedony *(plate 36)*. A new element is seen in the ornamental rows of pendants combining lotus and papyrus blooms and buds with round plaques. These motifs are also used in various forms as ornamental borders to the mural paintings in the rock tombs of the time.

The attempt to achieve the maximum unity of form, colour and often theme between the pectoral itself and the chain and fastener is very marked. The well-known rich 'rebirth of the god' pectoral, for example, uses the central motif of a scarab inlaid with lapis lazuli and two uraei several times over in varying arrangements in the chain as well. There is a similar compositional unity in the pectoral showing a new and a full moon in a boat *(plate 41)*. The lotus petals, which symbolize water, are repeated in the fastening, and the shape of the elongated beads in the chain repeat the inlaid drop pendants on the lower moulding of the pectoral. This unity is a faint echo of an ancient form in the shape of the hieroglyph *sa*.

A new feature in this connection is the asymmetrical arrangement in the pendant *udjat* eyes of Horus *(plates 34 and 40)*.

An important change, although in line with their previous development, also took place in the treatment of the traditional broad *wesekh* collars. It can be seen in the collars formed by the wings of the vulture goddess Nekhbet, made up of many rows of separate plaques shaped like stylized feathers and held together by tiny rings soldered on to each one, through which strings of beads were passed. The predominant note in the colour scheme is provided by the blue and red of the bird's body in the central section and the gold on its wings *(plate 45)*. A somewhat larger necklace with Nekhbet and Wadjet in the centre is arranged in the same way, and so is a smaller one with a Horus falcon.[35] The tips of the wings were joined by gold wire from which the usual type of counterpoise was suspended.

The large number of bracelets, found both on the arms of the mummy and elsewhere in the tomb, can be divided into four categories. In the first place there are those derived from the prototype bracelet of many rows of beads with spacers; the fundamental change here is that the fastening, which was originally merely a functional, if ornamental, element, has now become the central motif and the rows of beads serve only to secure the jewel to the wearer's wrist. On the bracelet in plate 55 the fastening takes the form of a scarab holding the king's cartouche in its front legs. Two other bracelets have circular fastenings of large lapis lazuli set in a broad granulated frame.[36] A more interesting variation is the bracelet made of seven pieces; three scarabs and symbolical motifs showing the hieroglyph *nefer* and an uraeus on the *neb* basket. On each side the pieces are held by six rows of small beads caught up in a fastening, inlaid with a locust *(plate 53)*.

The second category is that of the bracelets made in two solid halves hinged and fastened with a slip pin. The upper half is broader and ornamented either with a large semi-precious stone in an ornamental frame or with symbolical designs like the *udjat* eye, or the large lapis lazuli scarab seen on the bracelet in plate 54. The third category includes the thin metal bangles with a bead resembling the *seweret* or a symbol like the *udjat* eye. The fourth type of bracelet is the solid arm bangle ornamented either with alternating strips of different colours, or one-coloured inlaid stones.[37]

Ear-rings are usually rightly considered a foreign element in Egyptian jewellery, revealing a certain barbarization of fine taste. It is true that few of the examples which have survived are above the average level of taste. Nevertheless, the five pairs of ear-rings worn by Tutankhamūn when a child, and placed in a special casket in his tomb, show that Egyptian craftsmen knew how to treat in their own way this alien element, and these ear-rings owe nothing to the young monarch's other jewels. The heavy studs, calling for big holes in the lobes of the ear, may not be in keeping with our own taste, and the pendants attached to them are often over-heavy and over-ornamented, too. Yet taken simply as jewels, without considering the use to which they were put, they are magnificent examples of the art. There are three types in this group: studs without pendants, larger studs with a solid pendant in the shape of a pair of uraei *(plate 58)*, and three pairs of ear-rings made up of three parts, a stud, a solid pendant in the shape of a plaque or a hoop, and a row of small pendants on strings of beads *(plates 57 and 59)*. The pair with pendants shaped like ducks with spread wings deserve particular attention for the unity of style throughout *(plate 56)*.

The fertile imagination of the royal jewellers can be seen in the monarch's rings as well. Besides the simple types of scarab ring or rings with flat oval or rectangular bezels with relief ornament, they made much more intricate pieces involving many symbols combined in one design *(plate 60c)*. The most interesting example of this miniature sculpture is the bezel displaying a complete scene with six figures: Tutankhamūn praying to the sun, accompanied by a pair of Thoth's apes; the group is protected by the falcon of Horus and the vulture Nekhbet with outspread wings. This is certainly sufficient for one royal finger.[38]

The skills of royal jewellers were also used for larger works. The three coffins from Tutankhamūn's tomb, the small coffins containing the entrails of the deceased, and the innumerable objects brought from the royal palace or made especially for the funeral furniture, are all fine examples of the craft. The royal throne is also a magnificent piece of work, covered in gold leaf and inlaid with silver and coloured glass and faience *(plate 66)*. The royal couple depicted on the back of the throne *(plate 67)* wear several interesting jewels unlike any found in the tomb itself. Their crowns have circlet bases formed by rearing uraei with the sun, which the Egyptians conceived as a disk, on their heads. The king's crown is a richer variation of the *atef* type *(hemhemet)*, hung all round with uraei; the queen's consists of a pair of tall feathers framed by elongated horns with the sun in between them. Both wear broad collars covering their shoulders. A third *wesekh* hanging on a stand shows that it formed an almost complete circle, with a fastening shaped like a lotus bloom. The king's bracelets are of the usual type with bands of vertical coloured inlay, while the queen's right wrist is adorned by a gold bracelet with openwork spiral decoration. The king's belt is decorated with a fish-scale pattern inlaid with red, blue and white, repeated in the fringe below the clasp. Only his diadem has retained the archaic form consecrated by tradition, that of a ribbon tied at the back.

All the jewellery found in Tutankhamūn's tomb cannot possibly be included in such a general survey, but an analysis of the different types leads to some interesting conclusions which are worth summing up briefly. The traditional forms, used over and over again, are the vehicles for ever new variations in the ornament, and have, in many cases, parallels in contemporary murals. The 'open' form of pectoral developed considerably, and was often designed with the chain and fastening as a single composition. In almost all types of jewellery there are cumulative arrangements of different sacred and talismanic symbols which have superseded purely decorative elements. The jewellery on statues, figures and relief carvings in Tutankhamūn's tomb is, on the whole, far more conservative in taste than his real jewellery.

Characteristic of the way artists lagged behind contemporary reality is the jewellery on the figures of gods and men, and even on the sacred boats of various gods in the temple of Sety (Sethos) I in Abydos.[39] Besides the broad collar necklaces, there are pectorals with pendants such as were new in the time of Tutankhamūn.[40] The painted *wesekh* collars are both semicircular, with hawks' head fastenings, and almost completely circular and closed.[41] In the same way pectorals are shown both in the 'enclosed' architectonic form and in the 'open' form. Details of the symbolical designs on the pectorals are visible, as well as all the different types of chain on which they were worn. *Menat* necklaces, exclusively the prerogative of the gods, also appear, hung round the neck, thrown over the shoulder, or carried in the hand.[42] The monarch's fillet is still of the archaic form of that found in Tutankhamūn's tomb and worn by his predecessors too. The bracelets on wrists and arms are represented in the usual way. On the king's single, double and triple belts all the types of decoration are used; diamond and zigzag patterns, alternate strips of differing width, and scale ornament.[43] The goddesses and, in some cases, the gods as well wear archaic anklets on their feet.

Other paintings of the Nineteenth and Twentieth Dynasties are no more revealing in this respect. The changes in taste and fashion are seen only in a few details. The official representations in the temple of Sety I are perhaps even more conservative than contemporary murals in private tombs, for instance that of Userhet, where the paintings tell us much more reliably what fashions were at the time.

We do not know whether the women's fillets shown there were made of fresh flower petals fixed to ribbons, or were the work of jewellers; the broad ends of the ribbon are now turned forward from the bow at the back, and pass under the locks of the wig. Another form of this fillet worn by Userhet's mother and the women with her looks more like a cap, being broader at the sides, with more rows of ornament, covering the wig as far as the ear lobes.[44] The yellow colour of Kenro's wife's fillet, with the design in red, suggests that it was made of gold; the lower part is painted in blue and white, perhaps indicating that it was made of fresh flower petals, or even of cloth.[45]

Something like a return to the traditions of the Old and Middle Kingdom occurs as fillets are again worn by men; under the Eighteenth Dynasty they had been the prerogative of the ruler. The many-coloured three part fillet worn by Userhet appears to be the work of a weaver rather than that of a jeweller; Kenro, on the other hand, like his wife, is wearing a gold fillet, somewhat broader above the ears.[46]

The pectorals, which seem from the available evidence to have long been royal jewels only, are now being worn by high-born men as well. They are even combined with broad *wesekh* collars, attached to it by strings or chains. Userhet is wearing a pectoral with three hieroglyphs; *djed* in the centre and an *ankh* on either side. The many rows of lens-shaped flat beads are still in fashion. New elements in the arrangement of *wesekh* collars are shown in the murals but the details are not informative enough for us to be able to suggest how they were executed.

Both men and women wear bracelets, mostly typical forms, around their wrists.

Because the folds of the outer garment covered the upper arm, the second pair of bangles has been put on lower down, on the forearm. Only the monarch is shown with the second pair of bracelets in the traditional position on the upper arm.

Compared with the jewellery depicted on the walls of Userhet's tomb, that in the murals in the tomb of queen Nofretiti, wife of Ramesses II, is very conservative.

Individual statues also give us a certain amount of interesting and detailed information about jewellery. A granite statue of Ramesses II, in the Cairo Museum, shows, in low relief, a wrist-bracelet with the *udjat* eye, of the type found in Tutankhamūn's treasure. Ramesses is wearing a ribbon fillet adorned with an uraeus. A similar double version with two uraei above the brow is worn by a princess of his family whose statue is also now in the Cairo Museum. On the top of her head she has a crown of upright uraei with the disk of the sun on their heads, very like the wreath of uraei supporting the high crowns worn by Tutankhamūn and his wife shown on the back of their gold throne *(plate 67)*. There are large studs in the ears of the princess, and on her breast she wears a *wesekh* with the hieroglyph *nefer* repeated in the rows of beads. She has a bracelet on her wrist and in her hand a *menat* with a counterpoise representing the goddess Hathor, ending in a rosette. There are rosettes over her nipples on her tight dress.[47]

Unfortunately there has been no great royal treasure found to illustrate the jewellery of the Nineteenth and Twentieth Dynasties, comparable with the discovery of Tutankhamūn's tomb. The jewellery in private tombs shows no particular progress either in material or in technique, and new types are rare. Beads of various shapes were used both for bracelets and for necklaces, and the thick rows of lens-shaped beads were still popular, as their frequent appearance in contemporary paintings shows. The pendants are of very varied types: drop pendants, petals, lotus blooms, lilies, cornflowers, palmettes, rosettes, clusters of grapes, little vases and so forth, as well as talismanic amulets which are often in the form of miniature statues of the gods. The well-known traditional amulets are still in evidence: the *ankh*, the *udjat* eye, the *tit* (the so-called blood of Isis), the *djed* (the pillar of Osiris) and others. The ear-rings are mostly hoops either threaded into the lobes of the ear or fixed on like clip ear-rings; they are usually metal, but occasionally glass. Beads are still made of semi-precious stones, coloured stones and faience; coloured glass is rarer. Sometimes gilt wood takes the place of the precious metal, particularly where the jewellery had been made especially for the funeral furniture *(plates 72 and 73)*.[48]

Most significant of the new finds of royal jewels of this period is the pair of bracelets belonging to Ramesses II *(plate 69)*. They are solid bangles made in two parts, joined by a hinge, and resemble Tutankhamūn's bracelets in shape. The broader upper half is decorated with a pair of geese, or perhaps a two-headed goose, with its body set in lapis lazuli and heads, tail and frame in granulated work.

The jewellery of queen Tawosret dates from the end of the Nineteenth Dynasty.[49] Her fillet is unusually charming — a delicate circle of gold with large gold rosettes of ten petals fixed round it, their shallow chalices rather resembling poppies. Her necklace of tiny gold beads and pendant cornflowers is executed in a technique which recalls the filigree work of later periods. In their simplicity and skilled craftsmanship both these jewels are closer to the taste of the Middle Kingdom than to the almost 'baroque' taste of Tutankhamūn's day.

Far less aesthetic pleasure is given by the heavy ear-rings of Sety II, with their pendant cornflowers of different sizes,[50] or by the ear-rings of Ramesses XII, from the end of the Twentieth Dynasty *(plate 70)*. Although in general treatment they are not unlike Tutankhamūn's ear-rings, they lack firm compositional principles and elegance.

VI

THE LATE DYNASTIC PERIOD

Shortly before the outbreak of the Second World War the French Egyptologist and archaeologist P. Montet began the systematic investigation of the royal necropolis at Tanis; this has enriched the field by the valuable discovery of tombs of several kings of the Twenty-first and Twenty-second Dynasties. For the most part the tombs were intact, one of the few rare cases in Egyptian archaeology and indeed in Egyptian history altogether. Montet's discovery is no less significant than was Carter's in his day, although the funeral furniture of these later rulers is not as fantastically rich as that of Tutankhamūn. The jewellery discovered by Montet, however, forms a remarkable collection which gives us more exact and more complete information about the jewellers' art in the late dynastic period than any number of contemporary paintings could.[1]

As in the previous periods, here too there are many pieces of jewellery which in form and treatment remain firmly within the tradition handed down from one generation to another from the time of the Middle and even of the Old Kingdoms. In the first place there are the pectorals, both 'open' and 'enclosed' forms *(plates 74—76)*, almost all of which centre round one single motif, the winged or wingless scarab. In the enclosed type of pectoral the design often includes two goddesses, Isis and Nephthys. The open form uses either the winged scarab or the wingless scarab accompanied by uraei.[2] The first known pectoral of this type with a winged scarab is painted in a scene from a jeweller's workshop in the tomb of Nebamūn and Ipuky, dating from the time of Amenhotpe III. Unlike the winged scarabs of Tutankhamūn's treasure, which are heart-shaped, this type could be enclosed in a rhomboid shape. In the classic enclosed form of the pectoral a significant feature is the use of pendants to stress the vertical line; they are arranged in rows, using ornamental plant motifs or hieroglyphs, and sometimes hinged to the lower moulding of the pectoral.[3] This part of the pectoral includes two symmetrical symbolic scenes *(plate 74)*. A striking feature of all these pectorals is the change from bright colours and lively contrasts to cool greens and blue-greens, and even modified tones like grey-green, grey-pink, and so on *(plates 74 and 76)*.

Strangely enough the traditional form of the *wesekh* collar is not found among the necklaces, but only seen on the kings' gold masks, where it is indicated by chased and engraved lines.[4] The mummy of king Hekakheperrē Sheshonq is adorned with a broad collar in the form of a vulture inlaid with semi-precious stones, but unlike similar pieces in Tutankhamūn's treasure made of plaques, this is made in one piece.[5]

The three multi-row gold necklaces of Psibkhennē (Psusennes) are reminiscent of the type of necklace of large lens-shaped beads so popular from the Eighteenth Dynasty onwards.[6] Here it has developed into a new form of collar with a large and very intricately designed fastening. One of these collars is made of large lens-shaped beads; firmly fixed in rows of six, they form also a rectangular fastening adorned with pendant cornflowers on gold chains. Two other necklaces are made up of thousands of thin flat rings threaded so closely together that they form flexible gold tubes. The fastenings are slightly rhomboid in shape and are decorated with symmetrical patterns arranged round the central cartouche with the king's name, and completed by pendant cornflowers on chains. These pendants are an illustration, as it were, of the mathematical law of progression each chain ends in a cornflower, then divides, each new chain ending in a cornflower and then dividing, until a full tassel of innumerable cornflowers and gold chains is formed.

Single bead necklaces were also found in these tombs, as well as amulets. The three amulets in plate 77 are miniature gold statues of the goddesses Isis and Bastet.

The bracelets can be classified in several groups, following more or less the old traditions. The classical Egyptian form of many rows of beads with spacers is no longer found, but a pair of bracelets made in two hinged sections decorated with alternate blue and gold vertical bands comes close to it in the arrangement of the pattern, which is interrupted by a rectangular field in which an *udjat* eye is inlaid, on a basket *(plate 79)*. Other two-part bracelets are inlaid with hieroglyphic ornament. Another type of bracelet, composed of plaques with royal cartouches and loose segments is a development of Tutankhamūn's scarab bracelets *(plate 53)*, but linked with hinges *(plate 78)*. The third group covers both slender metal bangles and the heavy ones with hinged bezels. In the heavy types pegs are used to fix the crown between the ends of the metal band; this form seems to have been influenced by rings with a scarab turning on a pin. Not only is the execution similar, but motifs common in rings such as the scarab, the *udjat* eye, a bead (which is frequently used) and even in one case a Syrian cylinder seal are also used.[7] This type of bracelet already occurs in Tutankhamūn's treasure. The massive inlaid bracelet of Pinedjem is another variant *(plate 83)*.

Besides the traditional ring with a scarab turning on a pin, or some similar symbol, a new type of broad flat ring with the royal cartouche decorated in an incrustation technique appears *(plate 80)*. There are no ear-rings at all.

Apart from the collection of jewels worn by the monarchs during their lifetime, many jewelled articles made solely as funeral furniture were found in these tombs. They include the gold tips which protected the fingers and toes *(plate 81)* and the gold plates which covered the incision in the abdomen through which the entrails were removed during mummification *(plate 82)*. Only fragments of the bead shrouds of this period have survived, although a similar shroud of the Twenty-sixth Dynasty, found in Saqqara in the tomb of Tjanenhebu, has been successfully reconstructed from separate beads. It is joined to the dead man's gold mask and adorned with an archaic type of *wesekh* collar and a vertical band of gold plate inscribed with hieroglyphs. The kneeling figure of the goddess Nut finishes the band, and at the sides are the four sons of Horus; all are in beaten gold *(plate 85)*. The ornament on anthropomorphic coffins is arranged in a similar fashion.

The jewellery discovered in the royal tombs at Tanis represents the last great collection of royal jewels of the late dynastic era which are in general style and treatment still purely Egyptian. It is more difficult to form an impression of the art of the succeeding period. From illustrations of jewellery which have survived on statuary and in relief carvings it can be assumed that traditional *wesekh* collars, amulets, fillets, 'vulture head-dresses' for queens and princesses, bracelets and perhaps anklets as well continue to be made. Ear-rings and finger-rings are not seen as a rule. Men of high birth and position, and the monarch himself, wear jewelled belts. On the whole, however, the illustrations are more conservative than what was actually made and worn, and cannot be a reliable source of information. It seems certain, however, that the magnificent tradition of the jewellery making art was maintained right up to the end of the dynastic era in Egypt.

VII

THE END OF EGYPTIAN TRADITION

The Cairo Museum examples of jewellery of the Hellenistic and Roman periods of Egyptian culture shown in juxtaposition with Egyptian jewellery proper throw into clearer relief the differences between native and foreign treatments. The types of jewellery are the same; rings are still rings, necklaces necklaces, and bracelets bracelets, but the difference lies in the manner of working, the treatment of different materials, and the ornamental motifs used.

For the Egyptian craftsman a coloured semi-precious stone was simply either a means of making a given shape of symbolic significance, or else part of a larger unit in a cloisonné incrustation. With the exception of the beads used in necklaces, it is unusual for stones to be used for their own qualities, for their shape, colour and beauty, although Tutankhamūn's bracelets, for instance, are an exception. Lapis lazuli is the most suitable stone for the scarab, and when necessary Egyptian craftsmen used several pieces of stone of different shapes and sizes. Cornelian is used to represent the round sun-disk, or for amulets shaped like the heart. The craftsmen of Greece or Rome, on the other hand, were interested in the stones for their own sake; this is evident in the rings *(plate 90)* and in the bracelets *(plate 89)*. Some types of semi-precious stones, of course, are used for gem-cutting and as cameos, but cloisonné incrustation work is alien to Greek and Roman taste.

The snake bracelets in plates 86 and 87 were probably inspired by the cobra, yet they have nothing in common with the royal uraeus and the snake motif is never treated in this way in Egyptian jewellery. These royal cobras which twist their way round fillets and suns, and sink gracefully into baskets, never adorn the arms of the ancient Egyptians.

Certain techniques, for instance, the massive spirals of multiple gold wire, or the twisted wire common in classical jewellery, are rarely used in Egypt. Ear-rings of the Graeco-Roman period do resemble those found occasionally during the dynastic period, but the oriental influences which brought ear-rings to Egypt came from the same cultural focus which later affected the art of Greece. Fundamentally Egyptian jewellery is concerned with planes and colour, while the Greek and Roman conception is a three-dimensional one, treating colour as an additional touch to lend emphasis only.

The Egyptian and Graeco-Roman styles were undoubtedly too different to be capable of fusing in one Graeco-Egyptian or Romano-Egyptian style. The native tradition proved to be very resistant and no such style was formed on Egyptian soil. The further development of Egyptian jewellery can, however, be traced outside the country itself, in Nubia. The jewellery in the treasure of queen Amanishakete of Meroë shows that, in spite of unsophisticated workmanship, the Egyptian two-dimensional colour based approach to the art still survived in the first century A.D., as well as many symbolical elements such as the *ankh*, *udjat*, *djed*, uraeus, the head of the goddess Hathor, lotus blooms, relief carvings of Egyptian gods and goddesses, and so on. Classical forms of jewellery survived too, broad *wesekh* collars, and two-part bracelets turning on a pin and decorated with incrustation. The use of semi-precious stones for inlaying was the only technique to disappear, being replaced by cloisonné enamel. The motif of broad collar necklaces becomes an independent entity and appears in different variants often in hybrid combination with other symbolic elements, in particular on rings. The innate Egyptian sense of function in jewellery is now lost; previously it had been lacking occasionally, such as in the treatment of such an alien element as ear-rings. Now there are both 'shield' rings using the *wesekh* as ornament, and rings bearing the royal cartouche, the ornament being almost the breadth of a palm. The main difference between seal rings and those of the dynastic era is the circular form of the bezel.[1]

The last traces of the magnificent jewellers' art in ancient Egypt are found in the period from the third to the sixth centuries A.D., in royal tombs in Ballana and Qustul. The discoverer of the tombs, W. B. Emery, believes that this late peripheral culture in which the last glow of the glory of the pharaohs was dying out, was created by a group, which he calls 'X', drawing on the traditions of the Meroitic kingdom; the kings of this civilization ruled Upper and Lower Nubia for at least two hundred years.[2] The silver jewellery found in these Nubian tombs exhibits a synthesis of the plane-colour treatment of Egyptian art and the three-dimensional monochrome treatment of Greece and Rome. It is true that this synthesis was achieved in a provincial milieu and in a barbarian form. Nevertheless I believe that only in such conditions could it have been achieved at all.

Egyptian symbols are still seen in the ornament of the tall royal crowns: the ram of Amūn with the *atef* crown, accompanied by uraei; busts of Egyptian gods and kings carved in relief but, unlike Egyptian art, *en face*; relief carvings of Egyptian kings with the double crown on their heads and sacrificial vessels in their hands; rows of hawks; and so on.[3] These remnants of the Egyptian range of symbols are framed in decorative elements that come from classical antiquity, wave ornament and astragals. The semi-precious stones (of which cornelian is now the most popular) are treated in the classical and not the Egyptian style; it is their form and colour that are significant, not the symbol they are used to express. The large round, oval or rectangular cornelians on the kings' crowns are set in raised mouldings, so that they stand out from the metal background. The rectangular cross pattern characteristic of the arrangement of these jewels may perhaps be an echo of the Egyptian style of ornament. The prototypes of such pieces as the massive bracelets with geometrically stylized lions' heads, and the bracelet with a large, beautifully cut oval onyx, surrounded by beryls, amethysts and garnets in a symmetrical pattern, must be sought in classical and not Egyptian antiquity.[4] The same is true of the ear-rings, except where they make use of such Egyptian motifs as the *ankh* for pendants.[5]

Rings with flat crowns on a short stem recall one of the types worn in dynastic times.[6] Bead necklaces include all the types common to practically every period and locality; the beads are of the most varied shapes and arranged either according to shape or colour, or on the principle of alternating elements, or of grouping different elements to form a complex motif. An echo of the true Egyptian tradition can be seen in two necklaces with cornelian beads and silver pendants.[7]

This last and semi-barbaric echo of the great art of Egyptian jewellery in synthesis with trends from classical antiquity and perhaps from Byzantium as well, is an extremely interesting subject. Far more Egyptian elements can be traced here, than in the art of Egypt itself at this time. While Egyptian mythological ideas survive up to this period in Nubia, in Egypt they are superseded in the minds of the Christian Copts, who were the descendants of the ancient Egyptians, by Christian symbols and even, to a large extent, by ideas taken over from the mythology of Greece and Rome. Thus it is not Coptic art, but that of provincial Nubia, that carries on and inherits the art of ancient Egypt. This is what the situation appears to be in the field of jewellery; it is clear, too, that during the thousand years the two countries had been in contact Egyptian religious ideas and art had taken firm root in Nubia.

VIII

DECORATION IN EGYPTIAN JEWELLERY

While Egyptian jewellery is governed by the same general principles as all Egyptian decoration, it naturally has its own specific character, influenced both by the fundamental form of the different types of jewellery, and by the material and techniques employed. In general in almost all types of jewellery the form influences the choice of ornamental elements and the way they are arranged. In most cases this involves a strip arrangement rather than a spatial composition, so that Egyptian jewellers far more often use elements and motifs suitable for borders than those that need a broader composition. The only exceptions are the bead robes and shrouds of mummies, and the network of beads on goddesses' robes. It seems quite certain that this treatment, derived from the techniques used, originated in the jewellers' craft and passed thence into the idiom of the mural painters. The broad *wesekh* collars which cover a large area are nevertheless composed of single rows of beads joined together; they are not designed spatially at all. To some extent the collars in which spacers are used, where the 'breast-plate' is treated as a whole, can be considered an exception; unfortunately no original examples have survived and paintings tell us too little about the details.

The decoration of jewellery is also influenced by the physical factors mentioned above; the material and technique of execution. Over a large field the craftsman's purpose is served by ready-made components — beads of various shapes and colours. The threading of beads on a string is undoubtedly one of the most ancient forms of decoration, giving scope to a sense of form and colour in the choice and arrangement of the material. In most cases the jeweller did not arrange the necklace, but only provided the beads of semi-precious stones and precious metals. Faience beads were certainly produced in large numbers, as glass beads are today.

In all strings of beads it is the moment of choice that determines the quality of the necklace. Beads can be strung anyhow, as they happen to come to hand, or they can be sorted and a preference shown for a certain shape, colour and size for a uniform arrangement. Beads of the same shape, but different colours, can be strung in a fixed relation to each other as in the bracelet of gold and turquoise plaques in the shape of a palace façade from king Djer's tomb *(plate 2)*. Similar shapes can be combined with different sizes or the same or different colours for a parallel arrangement. Different shapes, sizes and colours can be strung together as in king Djer's bracelet of double beads combining two separate motifs. The arrangement can be paratactic, a simple or more complex pattern of two or more colours and shapes. King Djer's other two bracelets show more involved arrangement of phases of several groups of various ornaments. Symmetry is emphasized in both these bracelets, in the first by the choice of larger beads for the centrepiece, and in the second by the insertion of a distinct element, the gold rosette.

Later on this involved type of arrangement seems to have given way to a more simple treatment. The gold necklace of the Fourth Dynasty princess from Gîza *(plate 6)* is composed of a homogeneous series formed by the repetition of a single element. A triple motif of two elements in the order *a-b-a* was used for the fillet, as for the painted fillet of princess Nofret. There is, however, still too little evidence for us to be able to generalize.

In Egyptian jewellery, unlike other fields, a trend towards symmetrical composition can be seen very early. This is connected with the function of the various pieces of jewellery, for they could either reflect the natural symmetry of the human body, or strive to emphasize it. Any necklace, by its natural position, meets the first requirement, while symmetry can be further stressed by increasing the size of the beads towards the centre. The goal of symmetry is deliberately stressed in the case of bracelets, which until a late date, as shown both in actual finds and in mural paintings, are worn in pairs. The same is true of anklets, but only ear-rings have retained this feature up to our own day. In diagrammatic representation artists used the most common border ornament on bracelets, alternating broader and narrower strips; on the actual bracelets this effect was achieved by rows of beads and of metal spacers. The centre of the bracelet received no special treatment in the classical age of Egyptian jewellery, but a return to the symmetrical treatment found under the early dynasties does occur in the New Kingdom.

The centre of the fillet, above the brow, is often marked by the insertion of a distinctive motif; monarchs usually wear the royal uraeus, and queens and princesses either the vulture goddess Nekhbet or some other motif, such as the gazelle heads used on the fillets of the princesses from the harem of Thutmose III. Ordinary women wear a lotus bloom in the centre of their fillets. The band of the fillet itself is mostly decorated with the simple alternation of two elements: in ribbon fillets the alternation of two different strips; in wreath fillets or the ribbon-wreath combination, an alternation of two flower motifs (*e.g.* the fillet of princess Nofret, the two fillets of princess Khnumet on *plates 12 and 13*), or a homogeneous arrangement of a single element or motif (*e.g.* the fillet of princess Sithathoriunet on *plate 14*, and the fillet of queen Tawosret). These paratactic series are sometimes given a secondary symmetrical emphasis by the addition of a distinctive motif over the brow and perhaps another (most frequently a clasp with two papyrus blooms) at the nape of the neck.

The principle of simple series and alternations of colour is also the basis of composition in the broad *wesekh* collars; broader uniform rows of beads in various colours usually alternate with narrow rows of a single colour. The drop pendants are a distinctive feature which stress the symmetrical arrangement in their function of finishing off the collar. Not until the time of the Middle Kingdom does this traditional arrangement become less strict; various types of collars then develop, one example being the necklace of princess Khnumet *(plate 18)*, which has a symmetrical arrangement of symbolical motifs. Later on homogeneous and heterogeneous rows of beads alternate, incorporating components very different in shape and colour in an all-over composition.

Pectorals occupy a very special place in the development of Egyptian decoration. The architectonic frame of the 'enclosed' form led to the utilization of some common architectural forms in the ornament. These include the slender palm leaves breaking up the cornice which is borne in some cases on capitals of delicate columns ending in lotus blooms. In most cases, however, Egyptian craftsmen were content to use the usual border of alternate coloured rectangles of varying widths. Far more interesting are the heraldic compositions of symbolic significance which form the centre of the design. The reason for the choice of the mirror-reflection symmetrical arrangement was undoubtedly the placing of the pectoral and its relation to the symmetry of the human body, but the origin of heraldic designs goes back much further. They can be traced in the predynastic period and then from the Old Kingdom onwards in the grouping of relief carvings of the deceased on both sides of the false doors to the tomb. The first example of the use of this arrangement in jewellery is the clasp on the belt belonging to prince Ptahshepses *(plate 8)*; here the characteristic grouping is varied only in that the prince is shown seated and the centre of the design is occupied by an inscription with his name and title repeated twice. The same principle has been used in the composition of the pectorals of the Twelfth Dynasty in which the central motif is the cartouche with the king's name, sometimes with a fuller title. The symbolic scene into which the cartouche is inserted is an almost symmetrical design with only small deviations where the motif has its immutable traditional form or where the hieroglyphic forms necessitated it. This type of symmetry is used for the open pectorals, too, and was maintained right up to late dynastic times. The only remarkable deviation from the principle is seen in the pectoral of king Ahmose *(plate 22)*, where there are a number of unusual compositional features. Later pectorals in the form of the *udjat* eye are asymmetrical, as it does not lend itself to symmetrical treatment. The idea of using two eyes, common on steles, only appears once, on an 'enclosed' pectoral from the Middle Kingdom.[2] The richly ornamented 'open' pectorals of Tutankhamūn and some of those found in the royal tombs in Tanis made use of the same ornamental features as the borders of mural paintings of the time. Lotus blooms and buds on a pectoral with the full and new moon in a boat have their parallel in the broad borders of the murals in the temple of Amenhotpe III in Karnak, where the same arrangement of papyrus and lilies in used; and in tomb 82 where buds and blooms of the papyrus form the border.[3] The rich collection of pendants in the form of lotus and papyrus blooms, buds, and roundels, on other pectorals in Tutankhamūn's tomb, have parallels in many of the mural borders in Eighteenth and Nineteenth Dynasty tombs.

The Egyptian jewellers had at their disposal only a small selection of ornamental features. Undoubtedly the most frequent geometrical motif is that formed by alternating broad and narrow strips, useful for any type of border and for belts. The diamond and zigzag pattern is somewhat rarer, and occurs mainly in the decoration of belts. At a later date a scale ornament was also used. Other patterns do appear occasionally; the roundels ornamenting Tutankhamūn's fillet, the spiral which appears as a separate design in the necklace of queen Ahhotpe and in combination on the bracelet of queen Ankhesenamūn, in the scene depicted on the back of Tutankhamūn's throne. The most frequent plant elements are stylized lotus buds and blooms, papyrus and lily; separate lotus petals, cornflowers, various types of rosette and calyx, the fruit of the mandrake and dates. From the animal world sea-shells are common; the earliest examples were real shells, later replaced by shell-shaped beads in precious metals. Beetles, especially the *Scarabaeus sacer*, and rather more rarely flies and butterflies occur. A number of animal figures are stylized to suggest hieroglyphs: the hawk, vulture and ibis; the cobra and lizard; various fish and tadpoles; and besides the scarab, bees and locusts. This inventory is completed by a number of hieroglyphs of symbolic significance, which, from the Middle Kingdom onward, were used in groups or set in rows, particularly as pendants or as parts of a necklace. A large number of these traditional forms appear again and again in the Tutankhamūn treasure, but the designers reveal remarkable ingenuity in creating new variations in shape and colour and new groupings of immutable elements as hieroglyphs.

The Egyptian attitude to colour as revealed in their painting also influences jewellery, but colour in jewellery is also bound up with the use of coloured semi-precious stones. There are three whose colours fascinated the Egyptian craftsmen: red cornelian, pale blue turquoise, and dark blue lapis lazuli. The beauty and balanced compositions of these three colours can best be seen in the royal jewels of the Twelfth Dynasty. Occasionally pale green felspar is also included. Turquoise, in particular, was imitated in faience and later in glass. In Tutankhamūn's jewellery the colours are not always strikingly contrasted, but one basic tone is sometimes stressed at the expense of the others, as in plate 32 where dark blue dominates and lighter and darker shades of blue prevail in both the winged scarabs as well. In other pectorals, all the basic colours are used in gay succession: red, dark blue and turquoise, sometimes with green and orange as well. In some of the jewels, for instance the broad collar in the form of the vulture goddess Nekhbet *(plate 45)*, the colour of gold is strikingly used in the composition of the whole design, dominating the coloured incrustation. In the later dynastic era, represented by the royal jewels from the necropolis in Tanis, the trend away from warm, life-like colours to cool and shaded tones is characteristic *(plates 75* and *76)*.

IX

MATERIALS AND TECHNIQUES

Some writers have devoted greater attention to the materials used in the different arts and crafts in ancient Egypt, and to the methods of working these materials, than to the works of art produced. This is particularly true of Egyptian jewellery, and so I shall restrict myself to a summary of the most important facts.[1]

Of the precious metals gold was the prime choice for jewellery and other products of the jeweller's art and was, in the time of the Old Kingdom, less valuable than silver. It was one of the oldest metals known in Egypt, occurring in deposits associated with silver, copper and other metals, in the alluvial sands formed by crumbling gold-bearing rocks, or in veins. The gold-bearing region of Egypt is a vast area, stretching between the Nile valley and the Red Sea, and south to the borders of the Sudan, and Nubia seems to have been the centre of gold mining in ancient times. Its production rose during the Middle Kingdom, reaching its highest point under the Eighteenth Dynasty, and after a temporary fall it rose again in the second quarter of the first millennium B.C. The pale gold with a high proportion of silver in it is known by its classical name 'electrum'. Silver, often containing a high percentage of gold, was also known in Egypt from the end of the prehistoric era and was highly valued because there were no deposits of proper silver in Egypt itself, although by the time of the Middle Kingdom imports from Asia had begun to reduce its value. Both gold and silver were sometimes replaced by substitutes — gilt and silver-plated copper and bronze — and for 'funerary jewellery' gilt wood and plaster. Copper was mined in the eastern desert and possibly also in the peninsula of Sinai, and the ores necessary for the production of bronze were imported from the time of the Middle Kingdom onwards, apparently from Syria and western Asia.

Besides precious metals, semi-precious stones were much in demand for jewellery, as well as other coloured stones and later on various substitutes for them. The favourite semi-precious stones were cornelian, turquoise and lapis lazuli, followed by stones of a pale green colour like green felspar, sometimes referred to as amazon stone; purple amethyst was also used for beads. Cornelian was found in the eastern desert in the form of pebbles, being known before the dynastic era. In the Eighteenth Dynasty an imitation of cornelian was made by setting transparent quartz in red cement. Pale blue or green-blue turquoise was found on the peninsula of Sinai, but lapis lazuli was not native to Egypt and had to be imported, particularly from the time of the Middle Kingdom onwards, via Syria and other parts of the Near East. The main deposits were in north-east Afghanistan, but the stone was known and used for amulets from predynastic times. Transparent purple amethyst, used mainly for beads and more rarely for scarabs, occurred in Egypt itself, south-east of Aswan, north-west of Abu Simbel, and in the Safaga district of the eastern desert. Green felspar came from the eastern desert, near Gebel Migif, and was used for making beads as early as neolithic times. It is often seen in Middle Kingdom jewellery and was used for some of Tutankhamūn's jewels. Dark red garnet, found in the eastern desert, near Aswan, and in Sinai, was rarer, but appears mainly as beads, or as small details of the design. Of the various coloured forms of jasper the most usual was the red, found near the Hadrabia Hills, near Wadi Saga and in Wadi Abu Gerida. Green malachite, often confused with other green stones, was also found in the Sinai peninsula but was little used in jewellery. Milky translucent quartz and transparent rock crystal were chiefly used in the time of the Eighteenth Dynasty; the latter being also employed, as we have seen above, to produce imitation cornelian.

Alabaster and glazed steatite were made into beads, and green schist, basalt and black granite into scarabs.

From the time of the Ptolemaic dynasty coral and pearls were known, but mother-of-paerl and shell were common from predynastic times onwards. Ivory was also used in the jewellers' workshops, and in later times amber and other coloured resins.

The most important cheap substitute material was faience, which was made from predynastic times. The basic raw material was a white or brownish frit made from quartz sand, and glazed usually blue, green, blue-green or purple. The Egyptians also knew the secret of white, yellow, red and multi-coloured glazes. The glazes were of essentially the same composition as ancient glass, except for a lower lime and higher silica content, the colour being generally due to a copper compound. There are several types of glaze, of different colours and made by different methods, distinguished by their chemical composition.

One substitute for semi-precious stones, especially for turquoise, was glass, examples of which are known from early dynastic times, though these were probably produced accidentally. Glass was first made intentionally about the beginning of the New Kingdom, and was widely used in Eighteenth Dynasty jewellery. It then fell into disuse, and in the last millennium B.C. it was practically unknown in Egypt.

Metals can be worked either molten, in liquid form, red-hot or cold. Unfortunately very little is known about the techniques of metalworking in Egypt, and the primitive equipment used in Africa today has to serve as a guide. Rough tools were cast in open moulds, but for finer work, and particularly for statuettes, the *cire perdue* method was used. *Cire perdue* is a technique using wax and clay; in firing the clay hardens to form a model and the wax melts, its place being taken by metal. Red-hot metal was drawn, spun and hammered, using an anvil, hammers, tongs and bellows. This technique is best suited to iron, which was rarely used by Egyptian jewellers.[2] The various parts of a larger piece of work were soldered on, or joined by gold wire, stuck together with resin, and in the case of baser metals, riveted.

Much more important for Egyptian craftsmen were the methods of working cold precious metals and copper, beating, repoussé work (hammering the reverse side) and stamping. Cheaper jewels could be made by using thin metal plates and beating the ornament round a stone or hard wooden core or into a mould. The interior was then filled with plaster or some similar solid material. To make large quantities of small gold or silver ornaments with a relief design stamping was also used.

Fine details of a design on metal were either carved or engraved, which was simpler. The former called for the use of hammer and chisel, actually chipping the ornament into the metal, while in engraving the pressure of the hand on the graver was sufficient. The latter technique was used, for instance, for the line detail on the reverse of the royal pectorals of the Twelfth Dynasty.

Of the decorative techniques involving the use of different materials, both similar and dissimilar, the Egyptians were acquainted with damascening, the art of inlaying one metal with another, which was popular in the late dynastic period. They used the more precious of the two metals for the inlaid design, so that they would inlay copper or bronze with gold or silver; the softer metal was inlaid in the harder. For inlaying dissimilar materials, the incrustation technique, the Egyptians used coloured semiprecious stones and their substitutes, glass and faience. The typically Egyptian style of incrustation has similarities with the later cloisonné enamel technique, but differs from it in that stones or substitute materials were cut to the required shape and then cemented into the spaces between fences of gold strips soldered on to the foundation, which was usually of thicker gold. This cloisonné incrustation technique was prevalent in the Middle Kingdom and survived into the late dynastic era as the most important technique used by the jewellers of ancient Egypt. In some cases the gold fences themselves, which could be made thicker and variously shaped, played a part in the design. Occasionally the reverse technique was used; an ornamental motif in gold was soldered on to the base, and the background filled in with semi-precious stones cut flat. Some of the jewels of queen Ahhotpe *(plates 25 and 27)* show a combination of both these methods.

Niello work was another of the ways of inlaying metal known in ancient Egypt. It is not unlike cloisonné enamel but uses a special black substance, composed of metallic sulphides, instead of the enamel.

Granulation, decoration of tiny balls or grains, soldered or melted on to a gold base, is another ancient technique used from the time of the Middle Kingdom and extremely popular, particularly under the Eighteenth Dynasty. It has caused much discussion among modern craftsmen without any satisfactory solutions having been reached,[3] and it has been suggested that its origin was the region of the Aegean.

Among the other forms of decoration in Egyptian jewellery is the occasional use of simple interlacing patterns of gold wire, soldered on to a base. True filigree was unknown, but the pattern of gold wire and gold rings, soldered together, on the famous necklace of queen Tawosret comes fairly near to it. Gold wire was made either by drawing, or false wire by cutting thin gold plate into strips and removing the hard edges by beating. Jewellers used gold wire to make chains, most often using the 'colonne doublée' method. The ordinary 'colonne' is composed of rings folded into a double loop and put through the next; the 'colonne doublée' is a more complicated form of this which looks something like plaiting.

Gold and silver plating in Egypt was executed with thin metal foil beaten onto a metal base or glued on to wood or plaster. Amalgam and firing were plating techniques unknown in Egypt, and there is no evidence of the use of a similar process using a mixture of gold and lead powder applied to the surface with a fixative. To colour gold, particularly to give it a red hue, iron and copper were added, or the metal may have been dyed by means of some unknown organic substance. Coloured gold was favoured particularly in the time of the New Kingdom.

LIST OF ABBREVIATIONS USED IN THE NOTES

Altäg. Malerei:	A. Champdor, *Die altägyptische Malerei*. Leipzig, 1957
Anc. Eg. Paintings:	N. de G. Davies and A. H. Gardiner, *Ancient Egyptian Paintings*, I – III. Chicago, 1936
Ann. Serv.:	*Annales du Service des antiquites de l'Egypte*. Cairo, 1900 onwards
Ballana and Qustul:	W. B. Emery, *The Royal Tombs of Ballana and Qustul*. Cairo, 1938
Beni Hasan I, II:	P. E. Newberry, *Beni Hasan*, I, II. London, 1893
BIFAO:	*Bulletin de l'Institut français d'archéologie orientale*. Cairo, 1901 onwards
Carter, Tut-ankh-Amen	I, II, III: H. Carter and A. Mace, *The Tomb of Tut-ankh-Amen*, I – III. London, 1923, 1927, 1933
Cat. Gén.:	E. Vernier, 'Bijoux et orfèvreries' in *Catalogue général des antiquités égyptiennes du musée du Caire*. Cairo, 1907, 1927
Deir el Bahari:	E. Neville, *The Temple of Deir el Bahari*, I – VI. London, 1895 – 1908
Deir el Gebrāwi I, II:	N. de G. Davies, *The Rock Tombs of Deir el Gebrāwi*, I, II, London. 1902
Desroches Noblecourt:	Toutankhamon: C. Desroches Noblecourt, *Vie et mort d'un pharaon: Toutankhamon*. Paris, 1963
El Bersheh I, II:	P. E. Newberry, *El Bersheh*, I, II. London, 1893, 1894
Enc. phot. d l'art:	*Encyclopédie photographique de l'art, Le Musée du Caire*. Ed. 'TEL', 1949
Gizeh and Rifeh:	W. M. Flinders Petrie, *Gizeh and Rifeh*. London, 1907
Hassan, Giza I, II, III:	S. Hassan, *Excavations at Giza*, I. Oxford, 1932; II, III, Cairo, 1936, 1941
Hayes, Scepter I, II:	W. C. Hayes, *The Scepter of Egypt* I, New York, 1953; II, Cambridge, Mass., 1959
JEA:	*Journal of Egyptian Archaeology*, London, 1914 onwards
Keimer, 'Pendeloques':	L. Keimer, 'Pendeloques en forme d'insectes faisant partie de colliers égyptiens' in *Ann. Serv.*, XXXI – XXXIV
Massoulard, Préhist.:	E. Massoulard, *Préhistoire et Protohistoire d'Egypte*. Paris, 1949
Meir I – VI:	A.M. Blackman, *The Rock Tombs of Meir*, I – VI. London 1914 – 1953
Möller, Metalkunst:	G. Möller, *Die Metalkunst der alten Aetypter*. Berlin, 1924
Montet, Tanis:	P. Montet, *La nécropole royale de Tanis*, II. Paris, 1951
Reisner, Giza Necropolis:	G.A. Reisner, *A History of the Giza Necropolis*, II. Cambridge, Mass., 1955
Reisner, Mycerinus:	G.A. Reisner, *Mycerinus*. Cambridge, Mass., 1931
Royal Tombs I, II:	W.M. Flinders Petrie, *The Royal Tombs of the First Dynasty*, I, II. London 1900 – 1
Saqqara Mastabas I, II:	M.A. Murray, *Saqqara Mastabas*, I. London, II, London, 1937 (with K. Sethe)
Steindorff, Ti:	G. Steindorff, *Das Grab des Ti*, Leipzig, 1913
Temple of Sethos I:	A.M. Calverley, *The Temple of King Sethos I at Abydos*, I – IV, London, 1933-1958
Teti Pyr. Cem.:	C.M. Firth, B. Gunn, *Teti Pyramid Cemeteries*. Cairo, 1926
Tombeau de Ti:	'Le Tombeau de Ti', I – III, in *Memoires publiés par les membres de l'Institut français d'archéologie orientale du Caire*, Vol. LXV. Cairo, 1939 – 1953
Winlock, Lahun:	H.E. Winlock, *The Treasure of El Lāhūn*, New York, 1934
Winlock, Three Princesses:	H.E. Winlock, *The Treasure of Three Egyptian Princesses*, New York, 1948
Mace-Winlock, Senebtisi:	A.C. Mace and H.E. Winlock, *The Tomb of Senebtisi at Lisht*. New York, 1916
ZÄS	*Zeitschrift für ägyptische Sprache und Altertumskunde*. Leipzig, 1863 onwards

NOTES

CHAPTER I

[1] The Amratian finds are also referred to in the literature as Naqāda I
[2] Massoulard, Préhist., p. 39, pl. X
[3] Massoulard, Préhist., p. 121, pl. XXXIV
[4] Massoulard, Préhist., pl. XXXVI, 1
[5] Massoulard, Préhist., pp. 154 ff., pl. XLVIII, 20
[6] Massoulard, Préhist., pl. XLIX, 8
[7] Massoulard, Préhist., pp. 215 ff., pl. LXVIII, 8
[8] H. Frankfort, 'The Cemeteries of Abydos' in JEA, XVI, p. 214, pl. XXX, 1930
[9] W.M. Flinders Petrie, PREHISTORIC EGYPT, p. 41. London, 1920
[10] The 'wreath of justification' was found, for instance, on an empty sarcophagus in the pyramid of Sekhemkhet. (Z. Goneim, THE BURIED PYRAMID, p. 126. London, 1956)
According to recent opinion of M. L. Ph. Lauer, however, it is not a part of a wreath but a wooden lever left in the pyramid by the robbers after their operations

CHAPTER II

[1] Massoulard, Préhist., pp. 312 ff., pl. XCII, 2−5
[2] Royal Tombs II, pl. V, 19−21
[3] Massoulard, Préhist., pl. XCII, 4
[4] Royal Tombs II, p. 17, frontispiece
[5] Gizeh and Rifeh, pl. III
[6] Royal Tombs II, pl. XXXV, 81
[7] Royal Tombs II, pl. XII
[8] Several parts of jewels, made of gold, were found at Naga ed-Der and in the tomb of the queen Her-Neit at Saqqara. The first continue thematically in the predynastic development (shells, pendants in the shape of animals). A necklace was reconstructed from the golden and carnelian pearls of queen Her-Neit. Reconstruction which was done after iconographical documents is very reliable. But the value of original jewels is higher. (G. A. Reisner, THE EARLY DYNASTIC CEMETERIES OF NAGA-ED-DER I, Leipzig 1908, p. 30, pls. 6−9; W. B. Emery, GREAT TOMBS OF THE FIRST DYNASTY III, London 1958, pl. 99)

CHAPTER III

[1] Saqqara Mastabas II, pl. 1
[2] Saqqara Mastabas II, p. 3, pl. XXXVI
[3] Z. Goneim, HORUS SEKHEMKHET, pp. 13, 14, pls. XXXI, XXXIIa. Cairo, 1955
Z. Goneim, THE BURIED PYRAMID, p. 89, pls. 38, 48. London, 1956
[4] Reisner, Giza Necropolis, p. 2
[5] Reisner, Giza Necropolis, p. 46, pls. 37, 38
[6] Keimer, 'Pendeloques' in ANN. SERV. XXXIV, p. 124
[7] Möller, Metallkunst, p. 25
[8] Hassan, Giza II, p. 149, pl. LI, LII
[9] H. Schäfer and W. Andrae, DIE KUNST DES ALTEN ORIENT (Propyläen Kunstgeschichte II), p. 270 (1). Berlin, 1942
[10] Teti Pyr. Cem., p. 33, fig. 36
[11] Keimer, 'Pendeloques' in ANN. SERV. XXXI, pp. 145 ff.
[12] Hassan, Giza I, pls. LXXXVIII, LXXXIX

[13] Reisner, Mycerinus, Triad no. 9, pl. 39
[14] E.g. the necklace of Kaemheset (Cairo Museum. Enc. phot. de l'art, no. 41); the necklace of Ika (relief on the false door, Cairo Museum, reproduced in W. & B. Forman and M. Vilímková, EGYPTIAN ART, pl. 12, 1962); necklaces on reliefs in the tomb of Thiy (Tombeau de Ti I, pl. LXXII); and others
[15] Florence, Museo Archeologico, VI. Dyn. (reproduced in H. Ranke, THE ART OF ANCIENT EGYPT, no. 75. Phaidon, Vienna, 1936
[16] Reliefs in the tomb of Thiy (Steindorff, Ti, pls. 112, 114, 115, 118)
[17] Coloured reproduction: I. Woldering, EGYPT, pl. 15. London, 1963
[18] Keimer, 'Pendeloques' in ANN. SERV. XXXIV, pp. 124 ff.
[19] E.g. L. Borchard, DAS GRABDENKMAL DES KÖNIGS SAHURE, II, pl. XXXVI; Meir, IV. pl. VII; Meir, V. pl. XXVIII; Deir el Gebrawi, I, pls. III, IV, V
[20] G. Brunton, 'The Burial of Prince Ptah-Shepses at Saqqara' in ANN SERV. XLVII, p. 125; A.Y. Moustafa, 'Reparation and Restoration of Antiques: The Golden Belt of Prince Ptah-Shepses' in ANN. SERV. LIV, pp. 149 ff.
[21] Reisner, Mycerinus, pl. 63, no. 48 g—j
[22] Reisner, Mycerinus, Triad no. 9, pl. 39; no. 10, pl. 41; no. 13, pl. 45
[23] The stele of the lady Ihat, Cairo Museum, reproduced in W. & B. Forman and M. Vilímková, EGYPTIAN ART, pl. 23); Le Tombeau de Ti I, pl. VI; Saqqara Mastabas I, pl. XXIII, XXIV
[24] Le Tombeau de Ti, pl. VI; Saqqara Mastabas I, pls. XXIII, XXIV

CHAPTER IV

[1] Beni Hasan II, pls. XXVIII, XXIX: Meir V, pl. XIII
[2] P.A.A. Boeser, 'Das Diadem eines der Intefkönige' in ZÄS XLV, pp. 30, 31
[3] Deir el Gebrawi II, pl. XIX
[4] Deir el Gebrawi, I, pl. XIII; L. Klebas, DIE RELIEFS DES ALTEN REICHES, p. 85. Heidelberg, 1925
[5] El Bersheh I, frontispiece
[6] El Bersheh I, pl. XXXIII; Le Tombeau de Ti I, pl. XXXVI; this type is found from the Fifth Dynasty onwards
[7] Meir V, jeweller's workshop on pl. XVII
[8] Hayes, Scepter I, pp. 228 ff., 306 ff.
[9] Teti Pyr. Cem., pl. 23
[10] Hayes, Scepter I, 1 c
[11] Hayes, Scepter I, fig. 144
[12] Hayes, Scepter I, 1 c
[13] J. de Morgan, FOUILLES À DAHCHOUR, I—II. Vienna, 1895, 1903
G. Brunton, Lahun I, THE TREASURE. London, 1920;
H.E. Winlock, THE TREASURE OF EL LĀHŪN, New York, 1934;
A. C. Mace and H. E. Winlock, THE TOMB OF SENEBTISI AT LISHT. New York, 1916
[14] Mace-Winlock, Senebtisi, pl. XXI
[15] Meir VI, pl. XIX
[16] Hassan, Giza III, pl. LXXI, necklace from the mastaba of Hesi and Niankhhathor (W. M. Flinders Petrie, DENDEREH, pl. XXII. London, 1909
[17] El Bersheh I, frontispiece
[18] R. Engelbach, RIQQEH AND MEMPHIS VI, pl. 1. London, 1915
[19] Möller, Metallkunst, p. 49
[20] G. Farina, LA PITTURA EGIZIANA, pl. XXXV. Milan, 1929
[21] Meir II, pl. XV
[22] Winlock, Lāhūn, pls. VIII, IX

[23] Mace-Winlock, Senebtisi, pl. XXVII; Hayes, Scepter I, fig. 148
[24] C. Desroches Noblecourt, 'Concubines du mort et mères de famille du moyen empire' in BIFAO, LIII, pp. 7 ff.
[25] C. H. Stratz, 'Über die Kleidung der ägyptischen Tänzerinnen' in ZÄS, XXXVIII, pp. 149 ff.
[26] Cat. Gén. nos. 52022–3, 52050
[27] Winclock, Lāhūn, p. 43, pl. XI
[28] Möller, Metallkunst, p. 54
[29] Hayes, Scepter II, p. 20

CHAPTER V

[1] Cat. Gén. no. 52069
[2] Cat. Gén. no. 52670
[3] Hayes, Scepter I, pp. 306 ff.
[4] Cat Gén. no. 52073
[5] Deir el Bahari III, pl. LXXXII
[6] Deir el Bahari IV, pl. CIV
[7] Deir el Bahari IV, pl. CV
[8] Deir el Bahari V, pl. CXLV
[9] Deir el Bahari III, pl. LXIX
[10] Winlock, Three Princesses, pp. 3 ff.
[11] Hayes, Scepter II, p. 135
[12] Enc. phot. de l'art, no. 59
[13] Winlock, Lahun, pls. II, III
[14] Winlock, Three Princesses, pls. IX, X, XI
[15] Winlock, Three Princesses, pl. XVI
[16] Winlock, Three Princesses, pl. XVII
[17] Winlock, Three Princesses, pls. XX, XXI
[18] Winlock, Three Princesses, pl. VIII; Hayes, Scepter II, p. 131
[19] Anc. Eg. Paintings I, pl. XXVI; the ornamental fillet of beads was painted in the tomb of Paheri. (J. S. Tylorand F. L. Griffith, THE TOMB OF PAHERI AT EL KAB, pl. VI. London, 1899)
[20] Anc. Eg. Paintings II, pl. XXXIV
[21] H. Frankfort and J.D.S. Pendlebury, THE CITY OF AKHENATEN, II, pl. XXXVI. Oxford, 1933
[22] Cat. Gén no. 52674
[23] P. Barguet, 'L'origine et la signification du contrepoids du collier-menat' in BIFAO, LII, pp. 103 ff.
[24] Lange, AEGYPTISCHE KUNST, pls. 71, 72, Zürich-Berlin, 1939; Desroches Noblecourt, Toutankhamon, figs. 81, 82
[25] Anc. Eg. Paintings II, pl. LXII
[26] Möller, Metallkunst, p. 39
[27] Anc. Eg. Paintings I, pl. XXVI
[28] Anc. Eg. Paintings I, pl. XXVI
[29] Hayes, Scepter II, pp. 179 ff.
[30] Möller, Metallkunst, pp. 54 ff. Hayes, Scepter II, p. 186 a
[31] Möller, Metallkunst, pp. 39 ff. Hayes, Scepter, 1.C
[32] P. Fox, TUTANKHAMUN'S TREASURE, London, 1961; German edition: DER SCHATZ DES TUT-ENCH-AMUN, Wiesbaden, 1960; Desroches Noblecourt, TOUTANKHAMON
[33] Carter, Tut-ankh-Amen, II, pl. LXXV
[34] Besides the usual form Nebkheperurē there are variants: Nebkheperuiah, Hebkheperuiah. We cannot know how far they were the result of the artist's fantasy, and how far they may have had a certain significance with regard to the pharaoh
[35] Carter, Tut-ankh-Amen II, pl. LXXXI
[36] Carter, Tut-ankh-Amen II, pl. LXXXVI
[37] Carter, Tut-ankh-Amen, II, pl. LXXXII

[38] Carter, *Tut-ankh-Amen* I, *pl. LXVII*
[39] *Temple of Sethos I, pl. 7, frontispiece*
[40] *Temple of Sethos I, II, pls. 4, 11*
[41] *Temple of Sethos, I, II, pls. 19, 27*
[42] *Temple of Sethos I, I, pl. 20; III, pl. 45; IV, pls. 26, 35, 50*
[43] *Temple of Sethos I, I, pls. 18, 35; II pl. 12; III, pl. 44*
[44] *Altäg. Malerei, p. 125*
[45] *Altäg. Malerei, p. 177*
[46] *Altäg. Malerei, p. 177*
[47] *Enc. phot. de l'art, no. 143*
[48] Hayes, *Scepter* II, *pp. 394 ff*
[49] *Cat. Gén. nos. 52679, 52644*
[50] *Cat. Gén. no. 52397. In view of the large rosette motif the ear-rings and fillet seem to have belonged to the same set, although the fillet is of much greater artistic value.*

CHAPTER VI

[1] Montet, *Tanis* II, *p. 7*
[2] Montet, *Tanis* II, *pl. XXIX*
[3] Montet, *Tanis* II, *pls. CXIII, CXIV*
[4] Montet, *Tanis* II, *pl. XXI*
[5] Montet, *Tanis* II, *pl. XXIII*
[6] Montet, *Tanis* II, *pls. CVIII, CIX*
[7] Montet, *Tanis* II, *pl. XXX*

CHAPTER VII

[1] H. Schäfer, ÄGYPTISCHE GOLDSCHMIEDEARBEITEN, MITTEILUNGEN AUS DER ÄGYPTISCHEN SAMMLUNG DER KÖNIGL. MUSEEN ZU BERLIN, I, *pl. 21*. Berlin, 1910
[2] *Ballana and Qustul, pp. 5 ff.*
[3] *Ballana and Qustul, pls. 32 A, 32 B, 33A, B, 35 A, B, 36*
[4] *Ballana and Qustul, pl. 40*
[5] *Ballana and Qustul, pl. 41*
[6] *Ballana and Qustul, pl. 42*
[7] *Ballana and Qustul, pl. 48*

CHAPTER VIII

[1] *E.g. the group on the carved ivory handle of the knife from Gebel el-Arak*
[2] R. Engelbach, RIQQEH AND MEMPHIS VI, *pl. I*
[3] P. Fořtová-Šámalová and M. Vilímková, EGYPTIAN ORNAMENT, *nos. 289, 290*. London, 1963
[4] P. Fořtová-Šámalová and M. Vilímková, EGYPTIAN ORNAMENT, *nos. 301–305.*

CHAPTER IX

[1] *In his book* ANCIENT EGYPTIAN MATERIALS AND INDUSTRIES *(4th edition, London, 1962), A. Lucas gives an exhaustive account of the materials used in all the Egyptian arts and crafts. The working of precious metals and the jewellers' craft is dealt with by G. Möller in the book mentioned above,* DIE METALLKUNST DER ALTEN AEGYPTER, *where he gives a detailed bibliography of older works.*
[2] *Amulets and an iron dagger were found for example in Tutankhamūn's tomb;* Carter, *Tut-ankh-Amen* II, *p. 175, pls. LXXVII B. LXXXVII B LXXXII*
[3] *It seems that the mystery of this ancient technique may have been solved in 1933 by Littledale, who invented a new process of colloidal hard soldering.*

ILLUSTRATIONS AND CATALOGUE

For most of the jewellery which has already been published the numbers given here are those of the Catalogue Génerale of the Cairo Museum (Cat. Gén.), but the numbers of items from Tutankhamūn's tomb and Gīza were not accessible. The jewels of Tutankhamūn are therefore numbered as in Carter's original catalogue (Carter, Cat.); those from Tanis as in P. Montet, LA NÉCROPOLE ROYALE DE TANIS II (Montet, Tanis); and those from Gīza as in S. Hassan, EXCAVATIONS AT GIZA II (Hassan, Giza).

1 BRACELET

Gold, lapis lazuli and turquoise. Length 10.2 cm. Found at Umm el-Gaāb (Abydos) on the arm of a Thinite princess (W. M. Flinders Petrie, 1900–1901 excavations). Cat. Gén. 52011. First Dynasty

The bracelet is in two separate parts; it is formed by three rows of beads alternately of gold and turquoise, separated by large spherical beads of lapis lazuli through which the three strings pass. In the centre of the widest part of the bracelet there is a gold rosette of tiny petals bent inwards to the centre.

2 BRACELET

Gold and turquoise. Length 15.6 cm. Found at Umm el-Gaāb (Abydos) on the arm of the mummy of a Thinite princess (W. M. Flinders Petrie, 1900–1901 excavations). Cat. Gén. 52008. First Dynasty

The bracelet is composed of twenty-nine pieces of which fifteen are gold and fourteen turquoise. They are in the form of the *serekh*, the façade of the royal palace, and each is topped by a figure of the Horus falcon in profile. The pieces are the same on both sides, growing smaller towards the fastening. A double string is passed through every piece ending in the triangular gold fastening.

3 BRACELET

Gold, amethyst and turquoise. Length 15 cm. Found at Umm el-Gaāb (Abydos) on the arm of the mummy of a Thinite princess (W.M. Flinders Petrie, 1900–1901 excavations). Cat. Gén. 52010. First Dynasty

Two single beads of turquoise set in biconical gold tubes and threaded on a string alternate with three double beads of gold and amethyst (in one case replaced by a dark matt substance) fixed on the string, which lies in the central groove.

4 BRACELET

Gold, lapis lazuli and turquoise. Length 13 cm. Found at Umm el-Gaāb (Abydos) on the arm of the mummy of a Thinite princess (W.M. Flinders Petrie, 1900–1901 excavations). Cat. Gén. 52009. First Dynasty

The three rows of beads separated into three groups by three single beads through which the three strings pass. The design is symmetrical; the elongated beads are of spirally twisted gold wire, while the lapis lazuli beads are engraved with lines imitating wire.

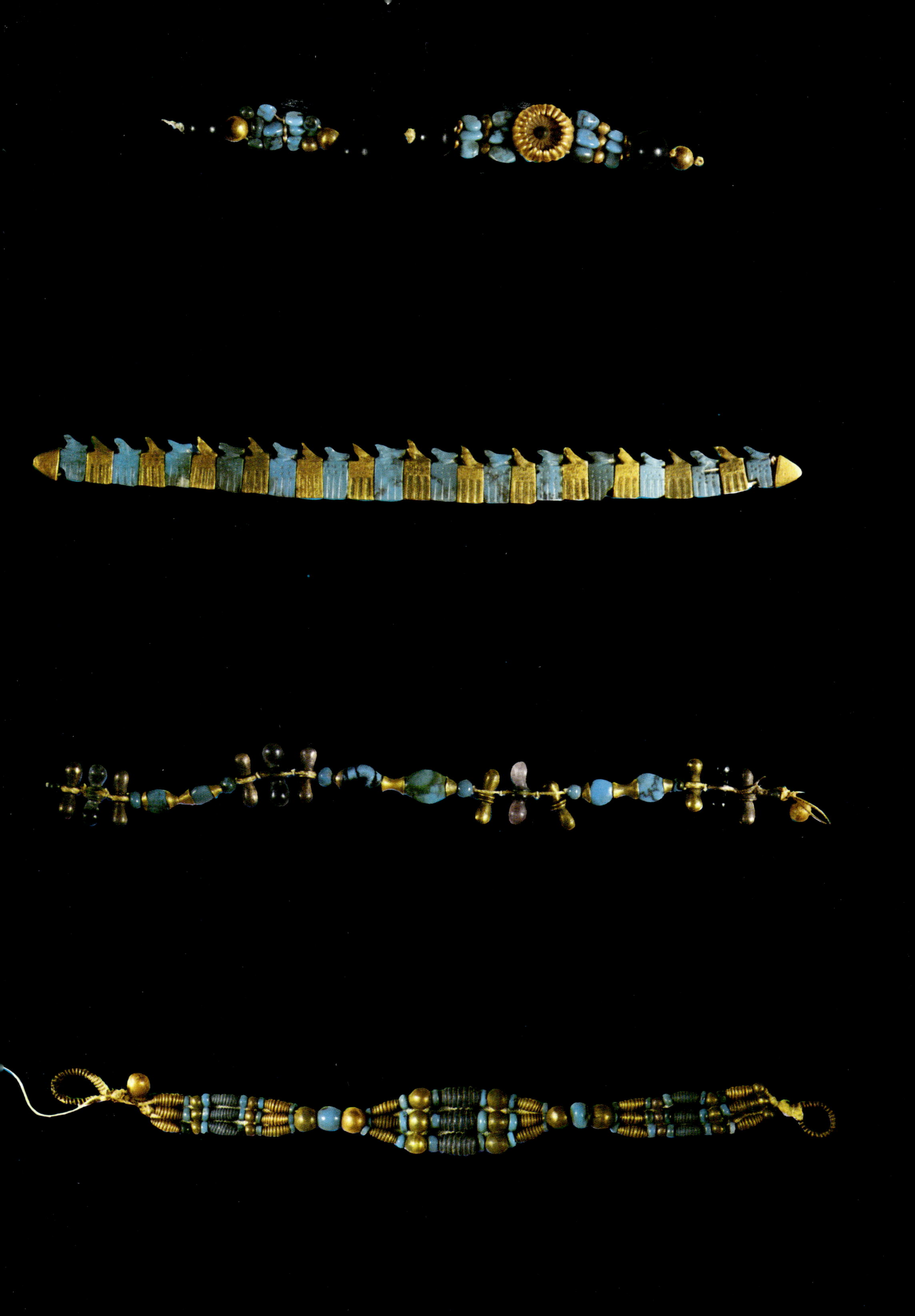

5 FILLET

Gold, copper and cornelian. Diameter 25 cm.; width of the band 38 mm. Found at Gîza, in the tomb of an unknown princess (S. Hassan, 1930—1931 excavations). Hassan, Giza, pl. LI, p. 149. Fourth Dynasty

The fillet consists of a band of gold, a rosette of beaten gold, with a design of four lotus buds in the centre, and on either side a double papyrus bloom joined by a flat disc of cornelian. The papyrus blooms form a nest for a pair of ibises whose beaks touch the tips of the flowers. A band of copper was fixed under the gold band by three copper rivets.

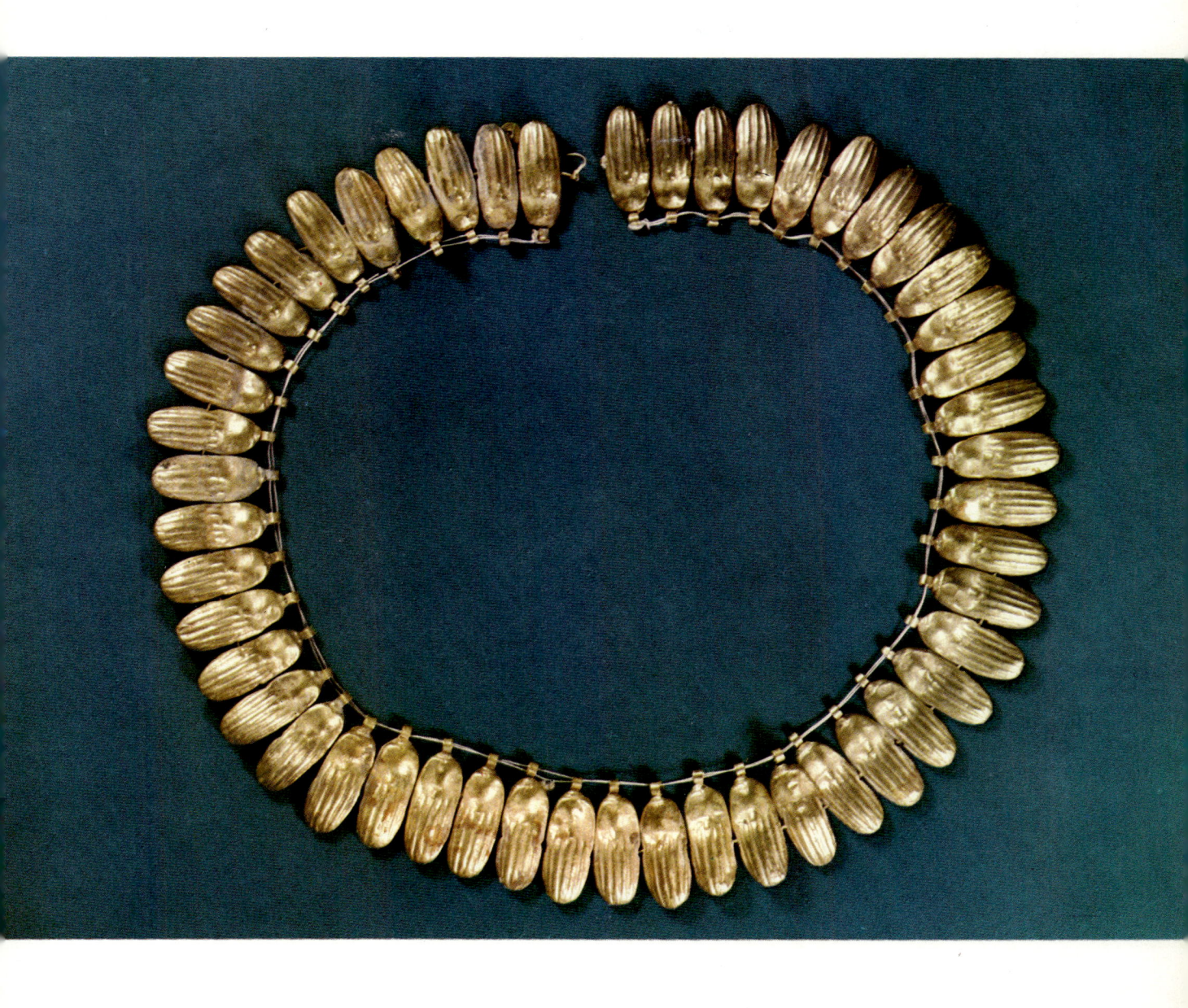

6 NECKLACE

Gold. Length of each bead 27 mm; length of the necklace *c.* 50 cm. Found at Giza, in the tomb of an unknown princess (S. Hassan, 1930—1931 excavations). Hassan, Giza, pl. LII, p. 139. Fourth Dynasty

The necklace, which was found on the neck of the mummy of the princess, consists of fifty beads threaded on two pieces of gold wire; the beads are formalized beetles *(Agrypnus notodonta)* sacred to the goddess Neith, probably the forerunners of the scarab (*cf.* L. Keimer, 'Pendeloques en form d'insectes faisant partie de colliers égyptiens' in *Ann. Serv.* XXXI, pp. 145 ff.). The gold wire is passed through a loop on the head of each beetle, and through each body.

7 BUCKLE (Detail of plate 8)

8 BELT OF PRINCE PTAHSHEPSES
 Gold, cornelian and blue and green faience. Length of buckle 10 cm.; width 45 mm.; length of belt 90 cm.; width 45 mm. Found at Saqqāra during excavation of the valley temple of the pyramid of Unis (Abdel Salam M. Husein, 1944 excavations). Cat. Gén. 87078. Fifth Dynasty

The belt consists of a gold buckle inlaid with cornelian and faience, and the belt itself of tiny beads on a gold base. The buckle is decorated with a scene in mirror symmetry, showing the prince on a chair, leaning on a tall stick. The prince's name fills the centre of the design, with a pair of falcons over it with spread wings, facing towards the prince. This scene is partly executed in champlevé incrustation and partly engraved on the gold base. The tiny gold and cornelian beads in a diamond and zigzag pattern forming the belt itself are threaded on gold wire, fixed in the gold tubes at the edge of the belt. At each end of the belt they are held by a semicircular fastening which covers the end of the bead pattern and is inserted in the buckle. At the back, the bead pattern is interrupted by a gold plaque which was used to fasten the symbolic tail in place. The belt was badly damaged, and was restored by Ahmed Yousef Moustafa in the Cairo Museum workshop 1947–1950. (Ahmed Yousef Moustafa, 'Repair and Restoration of Antiques: The Golden Belt of Prince Ptah-Shepses' in *Ann. Serv.* LIV, pp. 149–151).

9 PECTORAL OF SENWOSRET III

Gold, lapis lazuli, cornelian and turquoise. Height 61 mm.; width 85 mm. Found at Dahshūr, in the tomb of princess Mereret (J. de Morgan, 1894 excavations). Cat. Gén. 52002, Twelfth Dynasty

An enclosed pectoral with an architectonic frame. The cornice rests on slender pillars ending in lotus blooms, rising from a border of alternate broad and narrow rectangles. In the centre of the symmetrical design is a cartouche with the king's first name, Khakaurē. The two fantastic creatures with bodies of a lion and heads of a falcon adorned with a tall double feather, are symbols of the victorious monarch; beneath their feet writhe defeated Nubians and Libyans. Above the symbolical scene the vulture goddess Nekhbet, protectress of Upper Egypt, spreads her wings wide, her claws gripping the hieroglyph *shenu*, the symbol of universal rule. This pectoral is in openwork, with cloisonné incrustation; on the reverse the scene is engraved.

10 PECTORAL OF AMENEMHET III

Gold, cornelian, lapis lazuli and coloured glazed material. Height 79 mm.; width 10.4 cm. Found at Dahshūr, in the tomb of princess Mereret (J. de Morgan, 1894 excavations). Cat. Gén. 52003. Twelfth Dynasty

An enclosed pectoral in an architectonic frame with the typical alternating ornament of broad and narrow rectangles. The cornice is formed by stylized palm leaves. The centre of the heraldic composition is occupied by a double cartouche containing the king's first name, Nemarē, and titles. On either side the king himself is shown holding one of his conquered enemies by the hair with one hand while the second hand brandishes a club. The enemy, on one knee, is armed with a dagger and a throwstick. Behind the king is an anthropomorphic hieroglyph *ankh* (life) holding a feather fan in its 'hands'. The vulture goddess Nekhbet spreading her wings over the whole scene holds in her claws the hieroglyphs *ankh* and *djed*, symbols of life and continued being. The technique is the same as in the pectoral of Senwosret III (plate 9). The brownish green material on a white ground, partially flaked away, may perhaps be an imitation of turquoise.

11 PECTORAL OF AMENEMHET III

Gold, lapis lazuli, cornelian and some unidentifiable substance. Height 47 mm.; width 82 mm. Found at el-Lāhūn in the tomb of princess Sithathoriunet (W.M. Flinders Petrie and G. Brunton, 1914 excavations). Cat. Gén. 52712. Twelfth Dynasty

A trapeze-shaped open pectoral composed round the central motif of a cartouche containing the king's first name, Nemarē, supported by the seated figure of the god of eternity. On either side is a falcon, one claw gripping the symbol of universal power, the character *shenu*, while the other presses against the symbol for 'millions of years'. The disk of the sun on each of the falcons' heads is embraced by the body of a royal uraeus with its head touching the cartouche and the character *ankh* suspended from its neck. The border on which the whole composition rests is an alternating design of broad and narrow rectangles, the former inlaid with a zigzag pattern in cornelian.

An identically designed pectoral belonging to Senwosret II was also found in the treasure of this princess; it is now in the Metropolitan Museum, New York. (G. Brunton, Lahun I, *The Treasure*, pl. VI, XI, p. 29; H.E. Winlock, *The Treasure of El Lāhūn*, pls. VI, VII, pp. 29, 31.)

12 FILLET OF PRINCESS KHNUMET

Gold, cornelian, lapis lazuli and turquoise. Circumference 64 cm.; height of the upright motif 42 mm. Found at Dahshūr in the tomb of princess Khnumet (J. de Morgan, 1895 excavations). Cat. Gén. 52860. Twelfth Dynasty

The fillet is made of rosettes linking eight groups of three lyre-shaped calyces (two horizontal and one vertical) and a central rosette. Over the centre of the fillet, between two vertical calyces, is a golden vulture with outspread wings and the hieroglyph *shenu* in its claws. The details of the bird's body and wings are engraved on the metal. On the inner side of the fillet, at the back, there is a little tube to hold a spray of gold leaves.

The technique is openwork and cloisonné incrustation.

13 FILLET OF PRINCESS KHNUMET

Gold, cornelian, lapis lazuli and turquoise. Circumference 52 mm. Found at Dahshūr, in the tomb of princess Khnumet (J. de Morgan, 1935 excavations). Cat. Gén. 52859. Twelfth Dynasty

Six clasps hold a fine mesh of gold wire to which tiny five-petalled flowers and pairs of lapis lazuli beads are fixed; the flowers are of turquoise with cornelian centres. The clasps are shaped like rosettes with a round cornelian centre and four papyrus blooms inlaid with turquoise. The mesh consists of ten wires in three groups; each part is set with approximately twenty-six flowers and nineteen pairs of lapis lazuli beads. The delicacy of this fillet can be judged from the size of the different components: the rosettes are 25 mm., the flowers are 7 mm. in diameter, the beads less than 2 mm., and the wire is only 0.4 mm. thick.

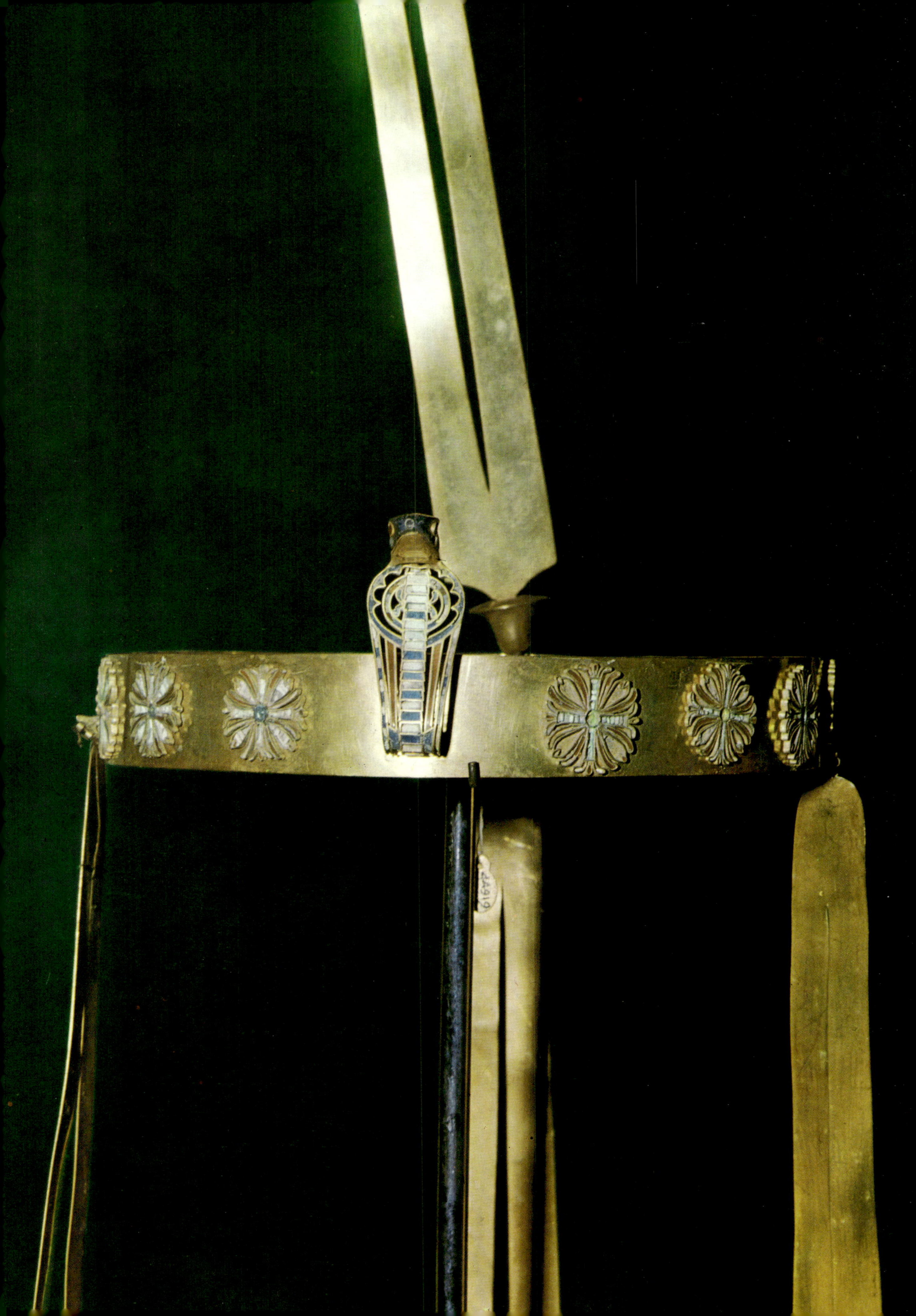

15 URAEUS

Gold, cornelian, lapis lazuli and green felspar or a pale green vitreous substance. Height 50 mm.; width 21 mm. Found at el-Lāhūn (W.M. Flinders Petrie, 1920 excavations). Cat. Gén. 52702. Twelfth Dynasty

This uraeus was originally part of a fillet or a royal crown; the head is carved from lapis lazuli, the eyes are of garnet. The treatment of the broadened part of the body is traditional, with the gold centre band engraved with horizontal lines, and passing into the base of the head. The heart-shaped upper part of the body is inlaid with felspar and lapis lazuli, the narrower lower part with cornelian. The undulating body is of beaten gold.

◀ 14 FILLET OF PRINCESS SITHATHORIUNET

Gold, cornelian, lapis lazuli and green felspar. Circumference 63.5 cm.; width of the gold band 28 mm. Found at el-Lāhūn in the tomb of princess Sithathoriunet (W.M. Flinders Petrie and G. Brunton, 1914 excavations). Cat. Gén. 52641. Twelfth Dynasty

This fillet is a band of gold 0.4 mm. thick, decorated with fifteen rosettes, each of four lily-like flowers inlaid with cornelian, lapis lazuli and green felspar or a vitreous substance. The place of the sixteenth rosette is taken by an uraeus with a head carved from lapis lazuli, eyes of garnet and an openwork body set with cornelian lapis lazuli and some damaged substance of the colour of felspar. Diametrically opposite, at the back of the fillet, a double feather cut from thick gold leaf is fixed in an ornament shaped like a papyrus umbel and tube and held by two rivets. At the back of the fillet and on each side a split pendant strip of gold capable of free movement is hinged on to the band.

16 SCARAB RING

Gold, lapis lazuli, cornelian and green felspar. Length of the scarab 16 mm.; width 11 mm. Found at el-Lāhūn in the tomb of princess Sithathoriunet. (W.M. Flinders Petrie, G. Brunton, 1914 excavations). Cat. Gén. 52689. Twelfth Dynasty

The head of the gold scarab is inlaid with lapis lazuli, the body with cornelian, and the wings with strips of lapis lazuli and green felspar. There is a hole running the length of the body, through which gold wire is threaded; the ends are then twisted together in a spiral fashion.

17a PENDANT

Gold and rock crystal. Diameter of the rosettes 24.5 mm.; of the medallion 21.5 mm. Found at Dahshūr in the tomb of princess Khnumet (J. de Morgan, 1895 excavations). Cat. Gén. 52975. Twelfth Dynasty

The pendant consists of a circular medallion in a gold frame, with three smaller pendants shaped like eight-pointed stars hanging from it. The medallion itself hangs from two rosettes with circular centres and eight loops round the edge. A recumbent animal (perhaps a long-horned cow) is painted in white on a blue background of frit, and protected by a thin sheet of rock crystal. The rosettes and small pendants are gold openwork with granulated ornament (cf.A. Lucas and G. Brunton, 'The Medallion of Dahshur' in *Ann. Serv.* XXXVI, pp. 197–200).

17b NECKLACE

Gold. Length 28 cm. Found at Dahshūr in the tomb of princess Khnumet (M. de Morgan, 1895 excavations). Cat. Gén. 52976. Twelfth Dynasty

The gold 'colonne doublée' chain is 2 mm. thick and made in four separate parts, to each of which are attached three pendants in the shape of formalized flies.

17c NECKLACE FASTENING

Gold. Width 27 mm. Found at Dahshūr in the tomb of princess Khnumet (J. de Morgan, 1895 excavations). Cat. Gén. 52977. Twelfth Dynasty

The fastening, attached to two fragments of a chain, is in the shape of a butterfly. The details of the body and wings are outlined in gold wire soldered on, and the spaces in between are filled with granulated ornament. The slip catch is on the reverse side, where the granulation is imitated by engraved dots.

17d NECKLACE WITH PENDANTS

Gold. Length 15.5 cm. Found at Dahshūr, in the tomb of princess Khnumet (J. de Morgan, 1895 excavations). Cat. Gén. 52978. Twelfth Dynasty

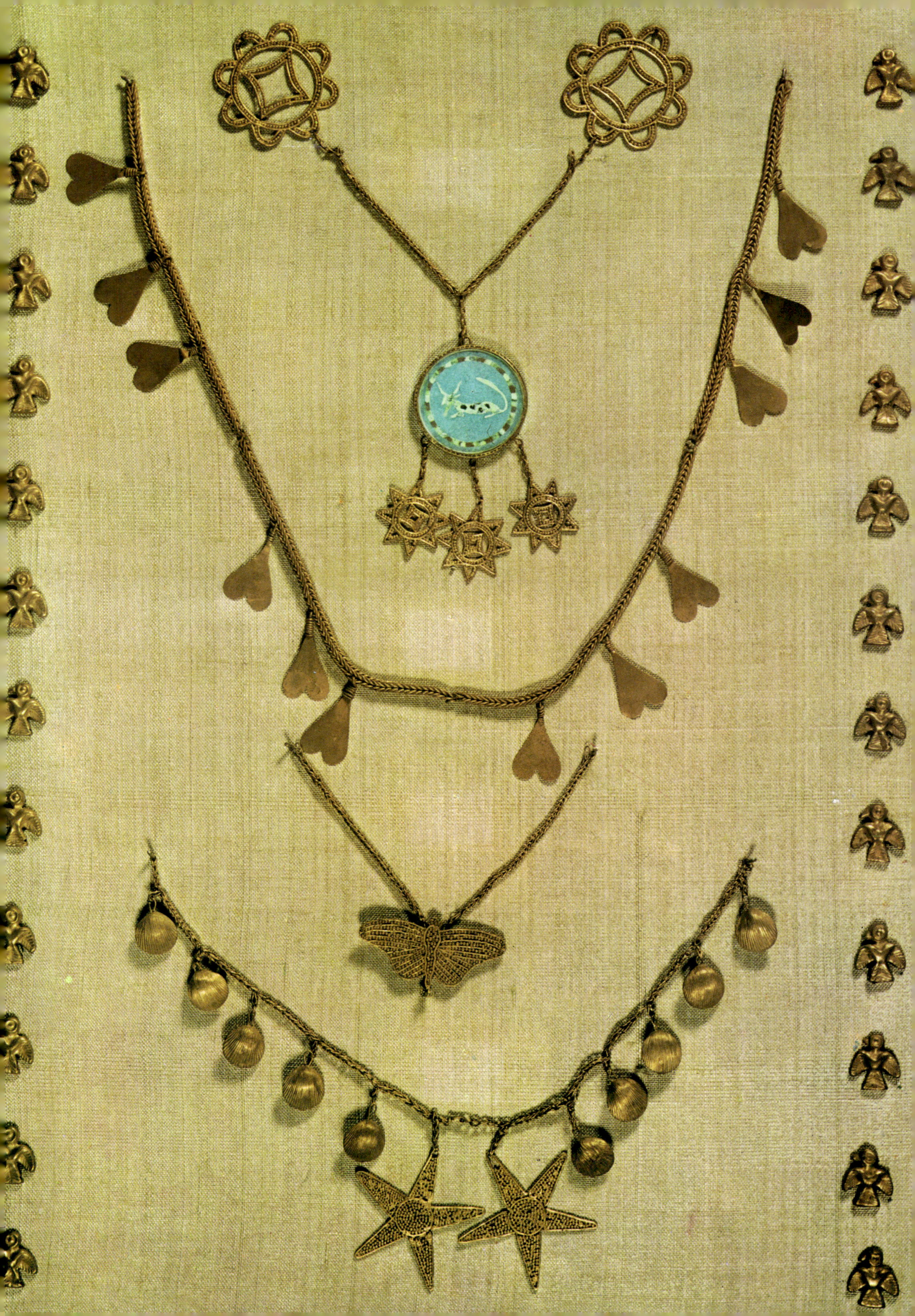

There are twelve pendants attached to this fragment of a 'colonne doublée' chain. The two in the centre are five-pointed stars in granulated technique with soldered wire outlining the centre and edge; the ten shell-shaped pendants at either side are made in two separate pieces and soldered together.

◀ **17e LITTLE BIRDS**

Gold. Height 11 mm. Found at Dahshūr, in the tomb of princess Khnumet (J. de Morgan, 1895 excavations). Cat. Gén. 52979. Twelfth Dynasty

These twenty-four birds are of beaten gold with chased details and smooth under sides. There are two openings in the lower part of each. They were originally sewn on clothes or attached to the hair of the wig, like the rosettes found in the tomb of Senebtisi (cf. A.C. Mace and H.E. Winlock, *The Tomb of Senebtisi at Lisht*, pl. XXI, pp. 18, 58).

18 NECKLACE

Gold, lapis lazuli, cornelian, turquoise and green felspar. Height of individual pieces 18–19 mm. A modern reconstruction of single pieces found at Dahshūr in the tomb of princess Khnumet. Cat. Gén. nos. 52920–1, 52919, 52973–4, 52965–6, 52959–60, 52961–2, 52971–3, 52929, 52931 52926–7, 52969–70. Twelfth Dynasty

The central motif in the design as reconstructed is the hieroglyph *ankh* on the mat *hetep*, inlaid with cornelian, turquoise and lapis lazuli. This symbol of life and peace is framed on either side by a jackal followed by a pair

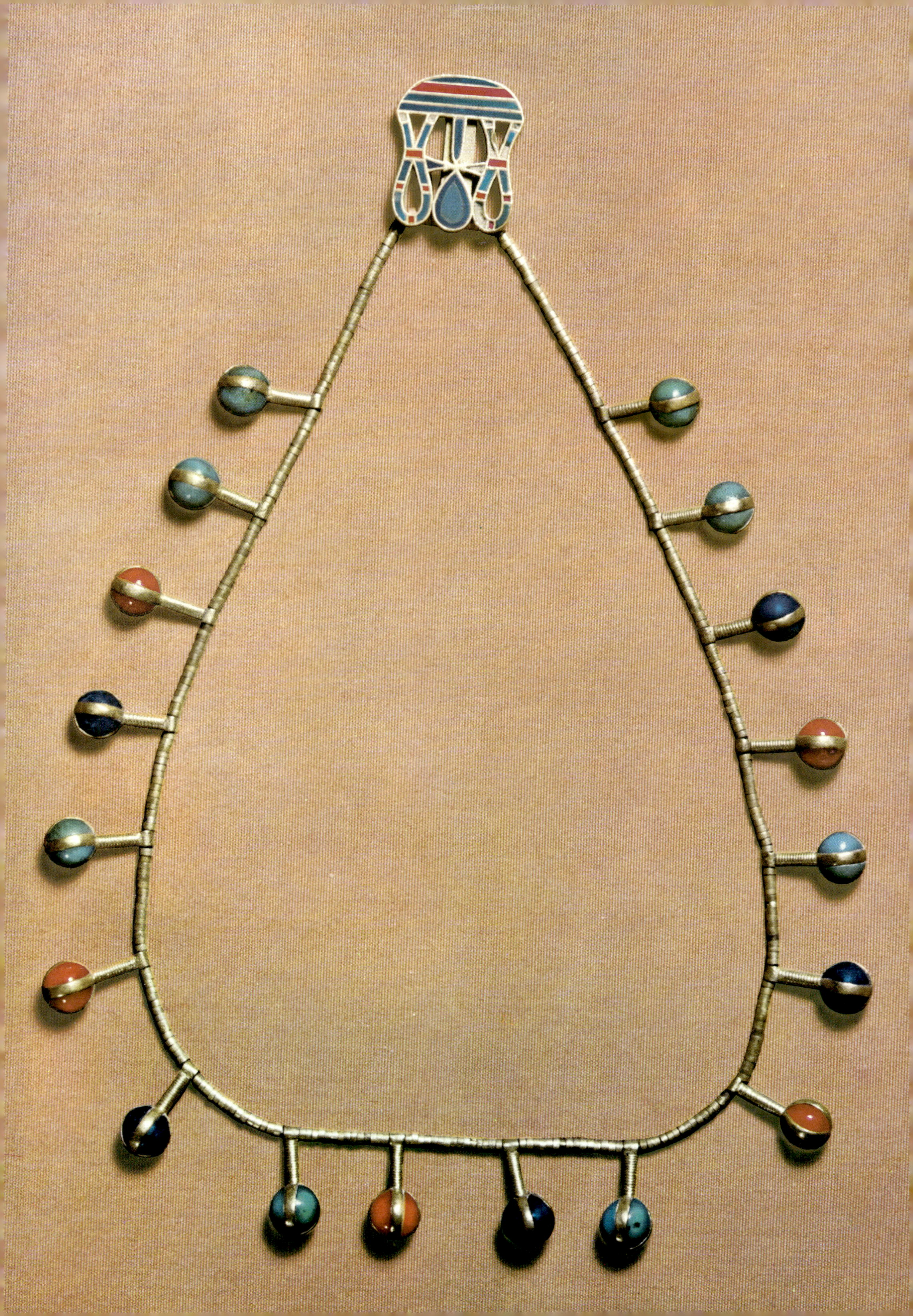

of vultures in baskets (the symbol of Upper Egypt), a pair of cobras in baskets (symbol of the goddess Wadjet, protectress of Lower Egypt), two symbols of the goddess Hathor, a pair of *udjat* eyes, two vases, two *djed* signs (the symbol of stability), two *ankh* signs (the symbol of life), two *sma* signs (the symbol of unity), and finally two bees, the symbol of the kings of Lower Egypt. The fastenings are shaped like two falcons' heads inlaid with lapis lazuli and green felspar, with cornelian eyes. A loop at the top and bottom of each figure holds them between two strings of tiny gold beads. The whole is completed by a row of drop-shaped pendants.

◀ **19 NECKLACE**

Gold, lapis lazuli and turquoise. Diameter of the beads 7 mm.; height of the fastening 19.5 mm. A modern reconstruction of pieces found at Dahshūr, in the tomb of princess Mereret (J. de Morgan, 1894 excavations), replacing the less suitable earlier reconstruction of the pendants hanging from a string of large amethyst beads. Cat. Gén. 53969, 53083. Twelfth Dynasty

There are eighteen pendants strung on a string of tiny gold beads; the pendants are of narrow bars of gold with lines engraved across them, ending in round beads of cornelian, lapis lazuli and turquoise, held in place by strips of gold. The fastening is composed of the hieroglyph *ankh* (life) in the centre with *sa* (protection) on either side, held in a *neb* basket. On the reverse, where the slip catch is fixed, the details are chased.

◀ 20   BELT (OR NECKLACE)
Gold. Length of individual shells varies from 49 — 57 mm. Found at Dahshūr, in the tomb of princess Mereret (J. de Morgan, 1894 excavations). Cat. Gén. 53074. Twelfth Dynasty

The gold cyprea shells are double, made of two separate halves soldered together. There are two strings threaded through each shell, with a single tiny shell of the same type threaded on each. This reconstruction suits a necklace rather than a belt, which would require longer spaces between the big shells (*cf.* H.E. Winlock, *The Treasure of El-Lāhūn*, pl. VIII).

21a   FRAGMENT OF A NECKLACE
Cornelian, lapis lazuli and green felspar. Length 80 mm. Found at Saqqāra (C.M. Firth, 1922 excavations). Cat. Gén. 52751. Twelfth Dynasty

A fragment of a necklace, comprising seventeen beads, mostly shaped like acacia seeds.

21b   BRACELET
Gold, lapis lazuli and green felspar. Length 19 cm. Found at Saqqāra (C.M. Firth, 1922 excavations). Cat. Gén. 52753. Twelfth Dynasty

The bracelet is made up of three groups of round beads of lapis lazuli and four groups of green felspar beads. The central group is separated from the rest by a pair of gold recumbent lions.

21c   NECKLACE
Gold, cornelian, green felspar and vitreous material (?). Length 33.5 cm. Found at Saqqāra (C.M. Firth, 1922 excavations). Cat. Gén. 52752. Twelfth Dynasty

Sixteen gold shells and ten tiny gold pendants representing a simplified form of the *udjat* eye are threaded on a string of small beads of cornelian, felspar, gold and a vitreous substance (?).

21d   NECKLACE
Amethyst. Length 34 cm. Found at Saqqāra (C.M. Firth, 1922 excavations). Cat. Gén. 52754. Twelfth Dynasty
A string of spherical beads of pale amethyst; the size decreases away from the centre (diameters 7 — 4 mm.).

21e   NECKLACE
Cornelian. Length 41.5 cm. Found at Saqqāra (C.M. Firth, 1922 excavations). Cat. Gén. 52755. Twelfth Dynasty
A string of spherical cornelian beads.

◀ **21f NECKLACE**
Garnets and vitreous material (?). Length 30 cm. Found at Saqqāra (C.M. Firth, 1922 excavations). Cat. Gén. 52756. Twelfth Dynasty

A string of garnet beads of which many (in view of the damaged surface) have been thought to be made of a vitreous substance.

22 PECTORAL OF KING AHMOSE
Gold, cornelian, lapis lazuli and turquoise. Height 72 mm.; width 92 mm. Found in 1859 in the tomb of queen Ahhotpe in Dra Abu el-Naga (Qurna). Cat. Gén. 52004. Early Eighteenth Dynasty

This is an enclosed pectoral in an architectonic frame with the usual alternating rectangle decoration. The zigzag pattern on the lower border represents water, on which the boat, which is part of the symbolical scene inside the frame, is floating. The monarch is accompanied by the gods Amūn and Rē, pouring purifying waters on his head. At the prow and stern of the boat are cartouches with the king's name; the two upper corners are filled in with falcons spreading their wings. To the right and left hand of the king large hieroglyphs declare that he is beloved of both these gods. The technique used is the same as in the pectorals of the Twelfth Dynasty, but the execution is not up to that level of craftsmanship.

23 CHAIN WITH THREE FLY PENDANTS

Gold. Length of the chain 59 cm.; length of each fly 67 mm. From the treasure of queen Ahhotpe, found in 1859. Cat. Gén. 52671. Early Eighteenth Dynasty

The gold chain of the *colonne doublée* type ends with a hook and eye. The three pendants are shaped like large, formalized gold flies; the wings and lower part of their bodies are simple flat pieces of metal cut to the required shape with a small thorax and two big eyes soldered on to them. The body is marked with pierced lines horizontal at the tip and vertical towards the head.

24 NECKLACE OF QUEEN AHHOTPE

Gold. Width 37.5 cm. From the queen's treasure, found in 1859. Cat. Gén. 52672. Early Eighteenth Dynasty

As reconstructed, this broad *wesekh* collar necklace has fourteen rows of small gold pieces, some rows ending in the fastening shaped like two falcons' heads and some in a row of gold roundels. Rows of geometrical forms (roundels, spirals and crosses) alternate with rows of zoomorphic motifs (lions, ibexes, antelopes, cats and winged uraei). The pendants forming the outermost row are shaped like simplified papyrus blooms. The falcons' heads are of beaten gold with an unidentified inlay, while the other pieces are stamped from sheet gold.

25 CROWN OF QUEEN AHHOTPE

Gold, cornelian, lapis lazuli and green felspar. Width 11 cm. Found in 1859, attached to the hair on the queen's mummy. Cat. Gén. 5264. Early Eighteenth Dynasty

The front part of this small crown is ornamented with double cable moulding, while the other half, rising in a narrow tongue, is inlaid with semi-precious stones. To the front of the crown is attached a moulded cartouche containing the name of king Ahmose in gold hieroglyphs on a background inlaid with lapis lazuli. The steep sides of the cartouche are decorated with squares of inlaid cornelian, lapis lazuli and green felspar, and the whole cartouche is flanked by two gold sphinxes in the round, their royal headdress *nemes* inlaid with lapis lazuli. The crown seems to have been assembled from pieces which were not originally meant to form a whole; the uniform conception so characteristic of Egyptian jewellery is lacking.

The identification of this piece as an unusual type of crown is by no means certain and most scholars would now agree that it is, in fact, an armlet.

26 BRACELET OF QUEEN AHHOTPE

Gold. Outer diameter 10.4 cm.; inner diameter 7.4 cm. Found in 1859. Cat. Gén. 52074. Early Eighteenth Dynasty

A large gold bangle of square cross section, decorated on the outer edges with a single trees pattern in gold wire. It is hollow, made of four similar-shaped pieces of gold plate soldered together. The queen had two pairs of these bracelets.

27 BRACELET OF QUEEN AHHOTPE
Gold, cornelian and lapis lazuli. Outer circumference 16.5 cm.; width 35 mm. Found in 1859. Cat Gén.. 52070.
Early Eighteenth Dynasty

This is the common type of bracelet made of beads threaded on gold wire and separated by spacers which, in this case, resemble gold beads joined together. The wires end in metal plates, two of which form the fastening, with a sliding pin hinge; the third is decorative and has the king's name, Ahmose, inscribed in hieroglyphs of gold on a background of lapis lazuli. The fourth plate was inserted into the fastening to enlarge the bracelet.

28 BRACELET OF QUEEN AHHOTPE
  Gold, cornelian, lapis lazuli and an unidentified green stone or vitreous substance (?) Diameter 66 mm.; height of the vulture 73 mm. Found in 1859. Cat. Gén. 52068. Early Eighteenth Dynasty

  The bracelet is made in two pieces with a hinged pin fastening. The front is ornamented with the figure of the vulture goddess Nekhbet with outspread wings; in her claws are two hieroglyphs symbolizing universal rule, *shenu*. The other half of the bracelet consists of two rounded bands of gold inlaid with stones separated by broad gold strips. There is a roundel inlaid with cornelian between the bands, and curving from it two stems ending in lotus buds, inlaid with turquoise. The bracelet is made in cloisonné.

29 AXE OF KING AHMOSE
  Gold, electrum, cornelian, lapis lazuli and turquoise or a vitreous substance of similar appearance (?) Length of the whole axe 47.5 cm.; of the blade 13.4 cm. Found in 1859 in the tomb of queen Ahhotpe. Cat. Gén. 52645. Early Eighteenth Dynasty

  The whole axe is covered with gold leaf. The blade is copper, the haft of cedar wood. Both sides of the blade are decorated with hieroglyphs inlaid in semi-precious stones. The side illustrated on plate 30 shows the god of time; the vulture goddess Nekhbet and the snake goddess Wadjet, with sprays of lilies and papyrus blooms as symbols of Upper and Lower Egypt; and the monarch himself in the shape of a recumbent sphinx. On the other side the king's two names are given in cartouches, the king himself is shown holding a conquered enemy by the hair and in the third band there is a griffn. The blade is fixed in the age-old manner, being bound by bands of gold to the haft, which is decorated with triple cross cuts which were also originally inlaid. On the spine of the haft there is a band inscribed with hieroglyphs giving the gull titles of the king. The elliptical end of the haft is ornamented with the symbolic plants of Upper and Lower Egypt and the character *nefer*, inlaid in semi-precious stones.

30 AXE OF KING AHMOSE (Detail of plate 29)

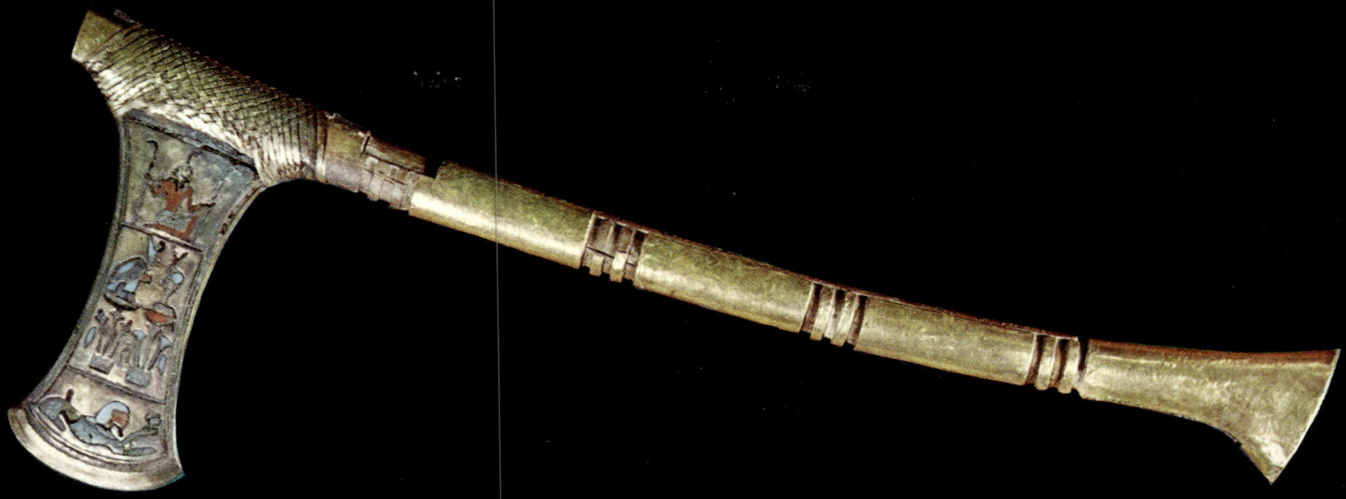

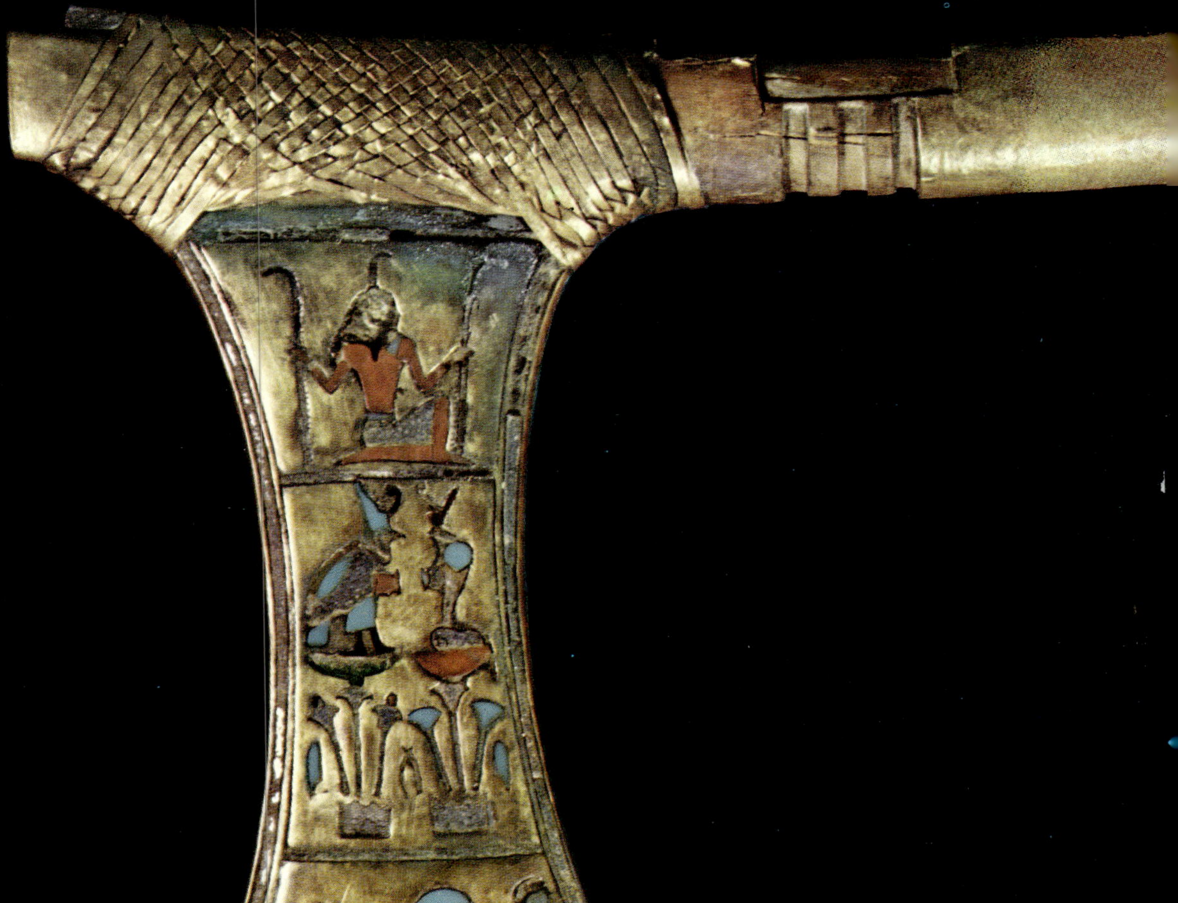

31 EAR-RINGS

Alabaster and a coloured vitreous substance (?) Diameter of the larger disk 30.5 mm. Found at Saqqāra (C.M. Firth, 1921 excavations). Cat. Gén. 52805. New Kingdom

These are button ear-rings with disks of different sizes. A hollow tube is fixed to the larger of the two, and the pin of the smaller disk fits into it. Both are slightly bossed on the outer side and decorated with a rosette of lotus petals arranged round a raised centre.

32 PECTORAL OF KING TUTANKHAMŪN

Gold, lapis lazuli, cornelian and glass. Height 65 mm.; width 11 cm. Found in Tutankhamūn's tomb. Carter, Cat. no. 256 PPP. Late Eighteenth Dynasty

The pectoral is in the shape of the vulture goddess Nekhbet, with spread wings and gripping a *shenu* hieroglyph in each foot. The head, neck and legs are of gold with the details engraved, while the feathers on the body and wings are inlaid with semi-precious stones and glass. The chain is made of alternating rectangular pieces of gold and lapis lazuli between two strings of tiny beads. On the reverse of the pectoral the details are engraved, with a cartouche containing the king's name on the neck of the bird. The chain is fastened by a slip catch with moulded figures of two hawks, also inlaid with semi-precious stones, on it.

33 FASTENING (Detail of Tutankhamūn's pectoral shown in plate 32)

Gold, lapis lazuli, felspar, onyx, cornelian and green glass. Length 36 mm.

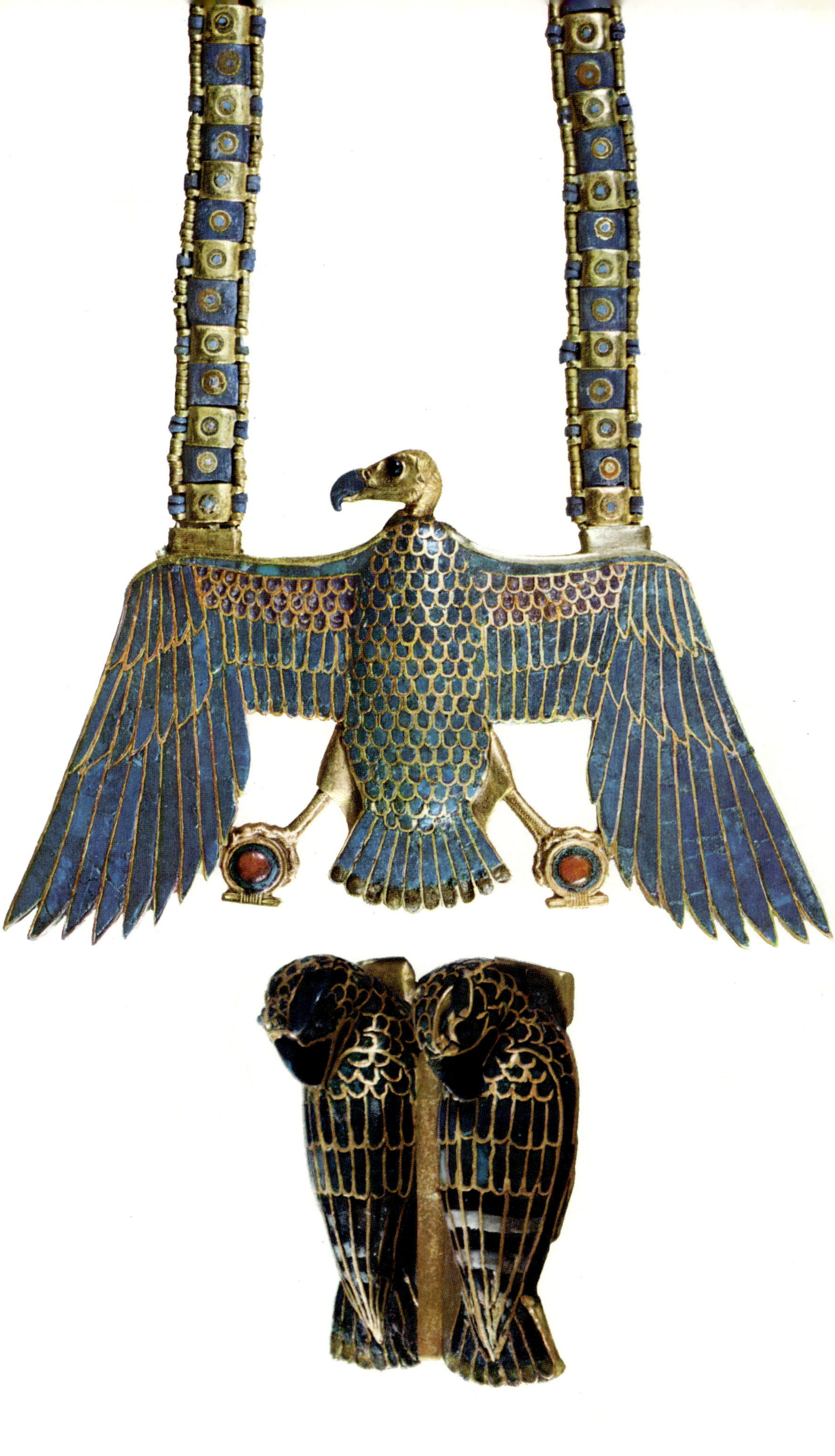

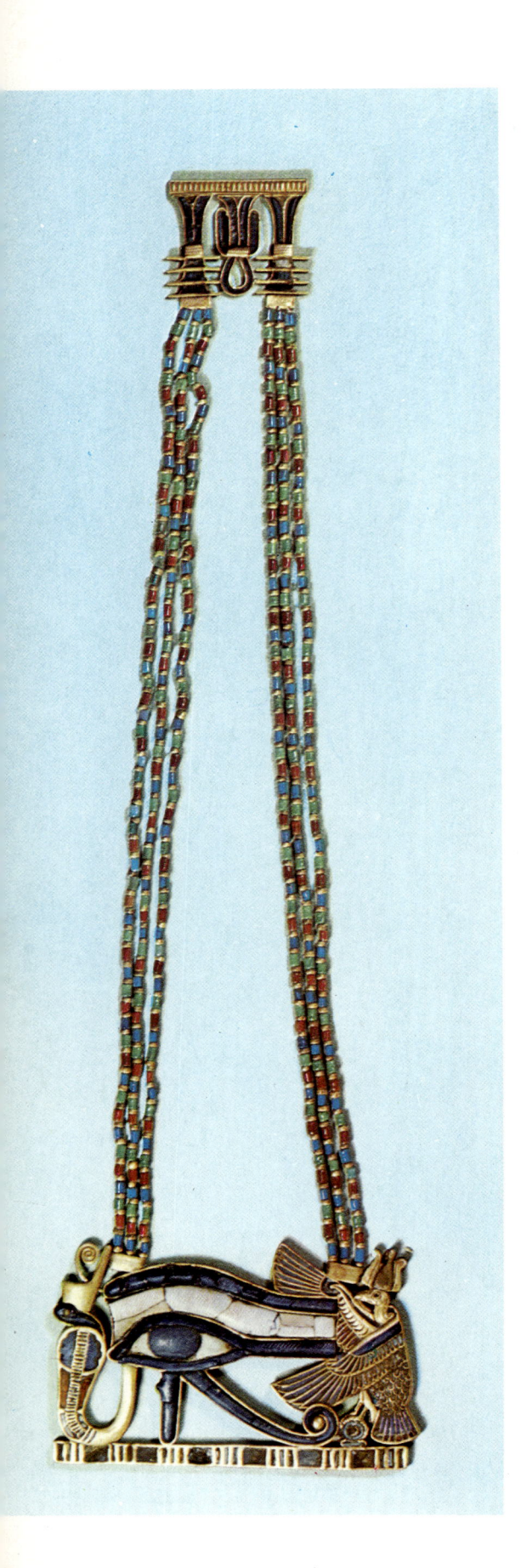

34 PECTORAL IN THE SHAPE OF AN *UDJAT* EYE

Gold, lapis lazuli, an unidentified green stone and coloured glass. Height 57 mm.; width 95 mm. Found in Tutankhamūn's tomb. Carter, Cat. no. 256 000. Late Eighteenth Dynasty

The *udjat* eye of Horus protected by a rearing cobra with the red crown of Lower Egypt on its head, symbol of the goddess Wadjet, protectress of Lower Egypt; and the vulture goddess Nekhbet, protectress of Upper Egypt, with the white crown of Upper Egypt on her head and a *shenu* character in her claws. The openwork pectoral with cloisonné incrustation decoration hangs from a triple necklace of gold, turquoise blue, bright green and red beads. The symbolical triple design of the fastening is composed of the hieroglyphs *tit* and *djed*, symbolizing life and stability.

35 PECTORAL IN THE SHAPE OF AN *UDJAT* EYE (Detail of plate 34)

36 PECTORAL WITH A WINGED SCARAB

Gold, silver, chalcedony, cornelian, lapis lazuli, calcite, obsidian (?) and red, black, green, blue and white glass. Height 14.9 cm.; width 14.5 cm. Found in Tutankhamūn's tomb. Carter, Cat. no. 267 D. Late Eighteenth Dynasty

The central motif in this unusually intricate design is a large scarab of greenish yellow chalcedony with inlaid birds' wings and gold bird-of-prey legs with the flowers symbolizing Egypt in its claws — on one side a lily, on the other lotus blooms. Its wings support a boat bearing an *udjat* eye guarded by two uraei. Above them rests a crescent, bearing a round plaque with the figures of Tutankhamūn, Thoth and Horus in relief. An ornamental row of pendants, representing lotus and papyrus blooms, buds and small roundels, hangs from the lower border of the pectoral.

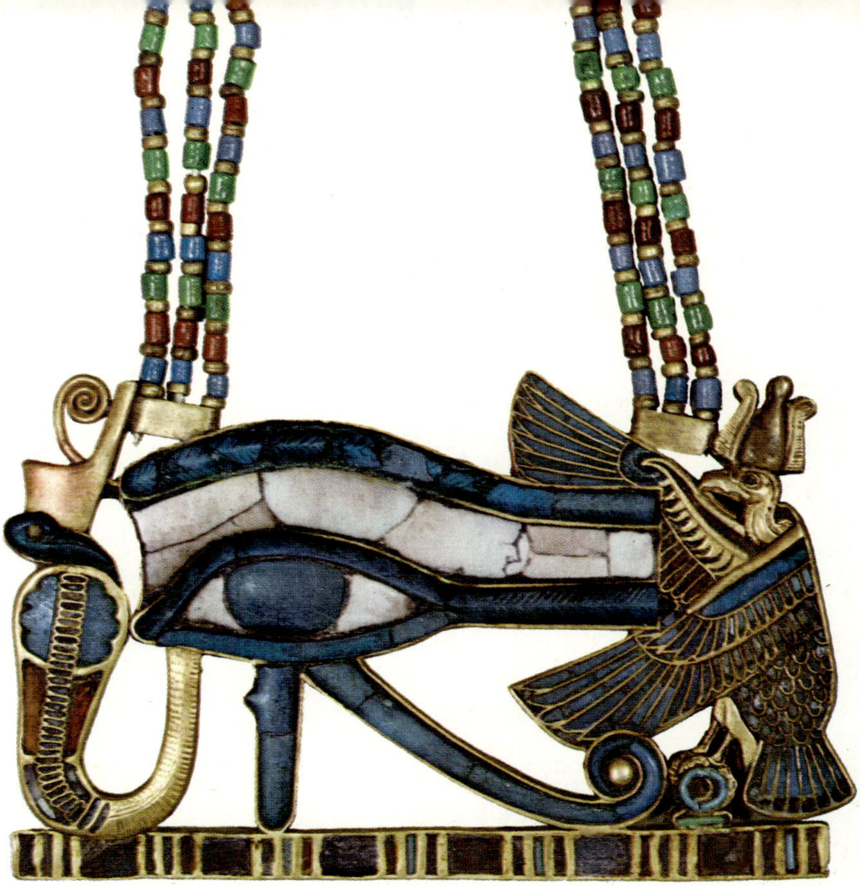

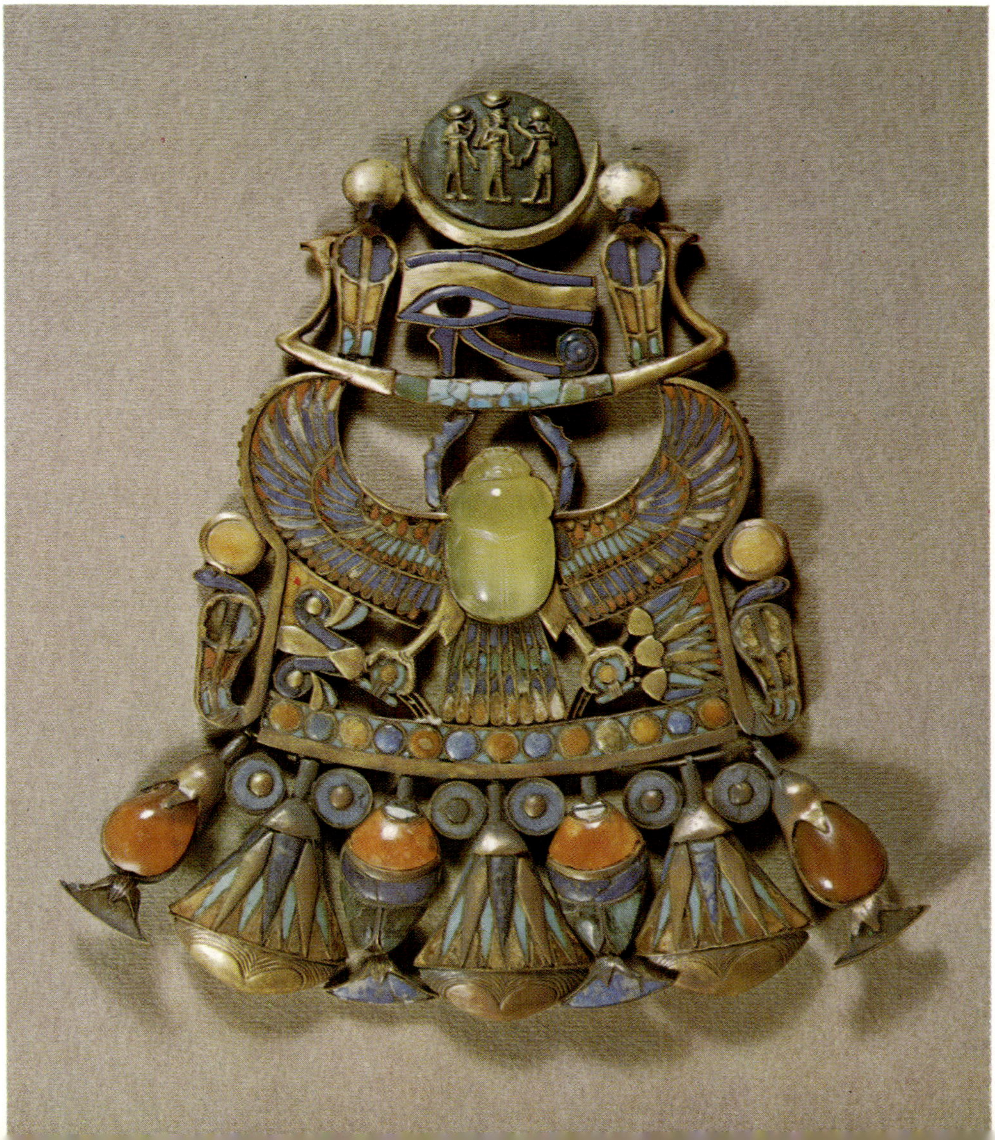

37 PECTORAL

Gold, cornelian, and blue and red glass. Height 16.5 cm.; width 24.4 cm. Found in Tutankhamūn's tomb. Carter, Cat. no. 261 M. Late Eighteenth Dynasty

In this variation of the enclosed pectoral, the frame comes to an end about two-thirds of the way up the sides; the top corners are filled in with coils of uraei writhing between roundels of cornelian. The central motif is a large greenish scarab with outstretched wings supported by the goddesses Isis and Nephthys, seated in the lower corners of the pectoral. Above the scarab are the royal cartouches and inscriptions to the two goddesses. The symbolical design is completed by the disk of the sun in the centre of the upper part with spreading wings. The pectoral is executed in openwork with cloisonné incrustation.

38 FASTENING (Detail of pectoral shown in plate 39)

The triple design of the fastening is made of two lotus blooms and a pear-shaped counterpoise bearing a cartouche with Tutankhamūn's prenomen and an uraeus on either side of it.

39 PECTORAL IN THE SHAPE OF A WINGED SCARAB

Gold, lapis lazuli, cornelian and dark blue glass. Height 90 mm.; width 95 mm. Found in Tutankhamūn's tomb. Carter, Cat. no. 256 QQQ. Late Eighteenth Dynasty

A winged scarab with a lapis lazuli body holds a golden crescent moon and bluish disk between its front legs and the tips of its wings. Below the scarab are three plural strokes and a *heb* basin. The separate elements in the design have various significances, but the whole must be related to the king's first name, Nebkheperurē; this unusual form is unexplained. The pectoral hangs from a 'colonne doublée' type gold chain held in engraved gold tubes; however the arrangement of the hinge attachment shows that it was originally meant to be worn on a three-string necklace.

40 PECTORAL IN THE SHAPE OF AN *UDJAT* **EYE**

Gold and blue faience. Height 60 mm.; width 88 mm. Found in Tutankhamūn's tomb. Carter, Cat. no. 256 RRR. Late Eighteenth Dynasty

Made of faience with a blue glaze, this pectoral hangs from a single string of cylindrical beads of blue faience and gold, some of them smooth and some with granulated ornament. A rearing uraeus guards the *udjat* eye, and the hieroglyph *sa* is placed beneath it on the inner side.

41 NECKLACE WITH PECTORAL

Gold, electrum, lapis lazuli, green felspar, calcite and glass. Height 11.8 cm.; width 10.8 cm. Found in Tutankhamūn's tomb. Carter, Cat. no. 269 K. Late Eighteenth Dynasty

The pectoral and necklace are designed as a whole. The pectoral, a row of lotus blooms and buds growing from the hieroglyph *pet* (heaven) represents the heavenly river on which floats a boat, bearing the crescent moon and the full moon between two flat plaques engraved with Tutankhamūn's cartouches and serving to hold the four-string necklace. The fastening is a rhomboid plaque decorated with an inlaid lotus bloom between two buds and two rosettes, and ending in a fringe of small blue and gold beads tipped with blue calyces.

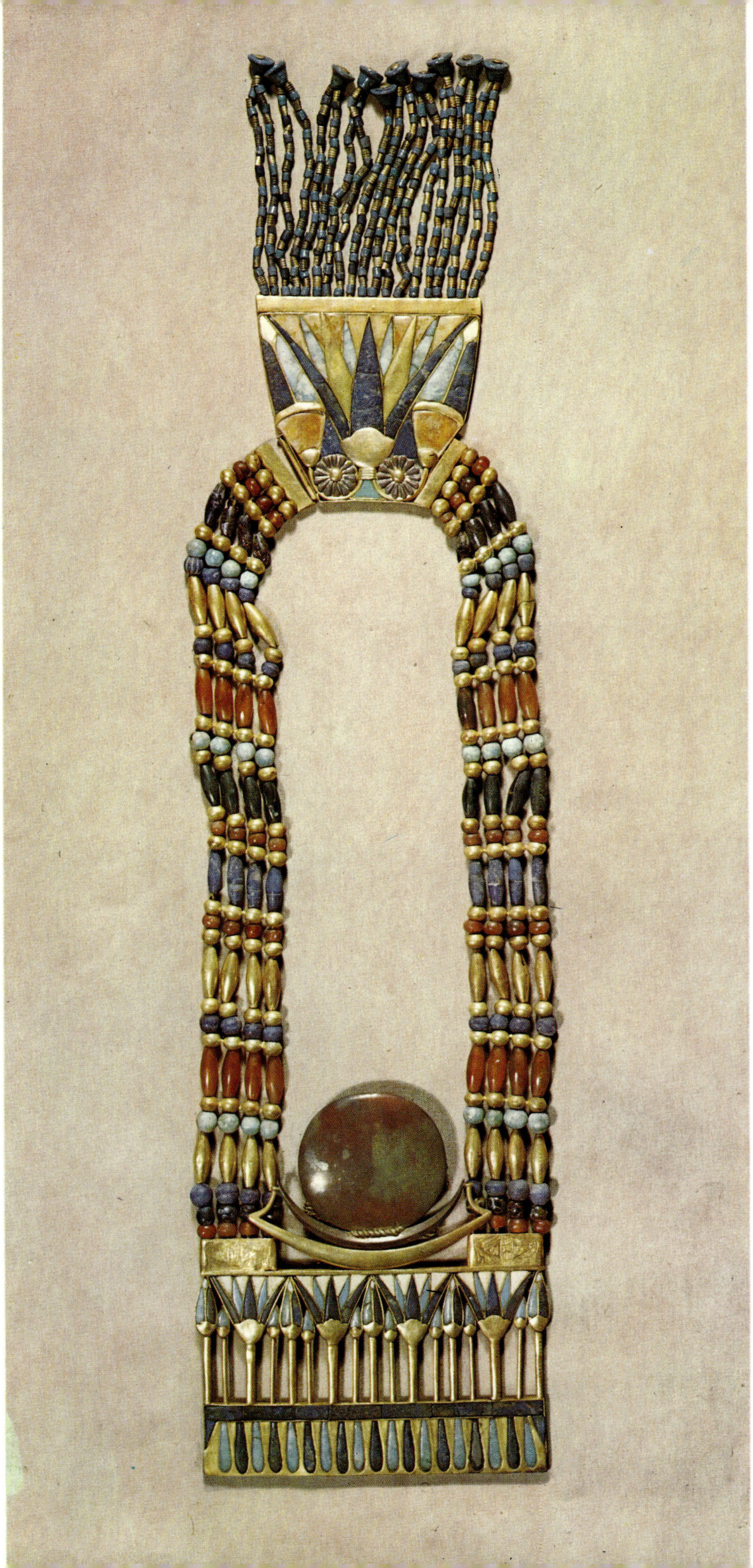

42 *DJED* PECTORAL

Gold, cornelian (or rock crystal set in red cement) and coloured glass. Height 12.0 cm.; width 16.3 cm. Found in Tutankhamūn's tomb. Carter, Cat. no. 261 L. Late Eighteenth Dynasty

This enclosed pectoral in an architectonic frame is capped by a double, unusually heavy cornice. The central motif which is the symbol of Osiris, the *djed* pillar with the sun disk on the top, is protected by the goddesses Isis and Nephthys with winged arms. Between their wings each has a cartouche with the king's names and an uraeus, one with a white and one with a red crown. The pectoral is executed in openwork and cloisonné incrustation.

43 PECTORAL WITH THE GODDESS NUT

Gold, cornelian and coloured glass. Height 12.6 cm.; width 14.3 cm. Found in Tutankhamūn's tomb. Carter, Cat. no. 261 P(1). Late Eighteenth Dynasty

An enclosed pectoral in an architectonic frame of wide and narrow rectangles inlaid in colour, and topped by a cornice. The centre is taken up by the figure of the goddess Nut with widespread winged arms; the background of gold leaf is engraved with the royal cartouches and an inscription referring to the goddess.

44 PECTORAL IN THE SHAPE OF TUTANKHAMŪN'S FIRST NAME, NEBKHEPERURĒ

Gold, lapis lazuli, turquoise, cornelian, green felspar and calcite. Height 90 mm.; width 10.5 cm. Found in Tutankhamūn's tomb. Carter, Cat. no. 267 A. Late Eighteenth Dynasty

A winged scarab with a body inlaid with lapis lazuli holds between its front legs a sun-disk inlaid in cornelian. The three plural marks are also in cornelian, while the *neb* basket is turquoise. The wings form the shape of a heart.

45 COLLAR NECKLACE IN THE SHAPE OF THE VULTURE GODDESS NEKHBET

Gold and coloured glass. Height (including wings) 36.5 cm.; width (ditto) 46.5 cm. Found in Tutankhamūn's tomb. Carter, Cat. no. 256 MMM. Late Eighteenth Dynasty

This broad collar necklace in the form of the vulture goddess with long curving wings consists of 256 pieces inlaid with glass of turquoise, red and greenish colour. Shape and colour are defined by gold cells; at the centre the colours are bright, predominantly turquoise blue and red, and towards the tip of the wings gold predominates.

46 PECTORAL IN THE SHAPE OF A *BA* BIRD
Gold, turquoise, lapis lazuli and cornelian. Height 12.5 cm.; width 33 cm. Found in Tutankhamūn's tomb. Carter, Cat. no. 256 B2. Late Eighteenth Dynasty

This bird with widespread wings and a human head is the Egyptian concept of the human soul — *ba*. The head is a miniature portrait of the young pharaoh. The upper part of its body is adorned with a broad *wesekh* collar and its claws hold the character for universal power, *shenu*. This pectoral was made as funeral furniture.

47 HEAD OF TUTANKHAMŪN (Detail of pectoral shown in plate 46)

48 PECTORAL WITH A WINGED SCARAB

Gold, silver, electrum, lapis lazuli, cornelian, calcite, green felspar, obsidian (?) and white, blue, green and black glass. Height 12.5 cm.; width 13 cm. Found in Tutankhamūn's tomb. Carter, Cat. no. 267 N. Late Eighteenth Dynasty

An open pectoral with a heraldic design built up on a narrow moulding inlaid with small roundels; in the centre is a winged scarab with an uraeus on either side. The scarab holds a crescent and full moon between its front legs, and below its body there are plural signs and a *neb* basket. The whole design centres on the first name of the monarch, Nebkheperurē. The triangular corners between the scarab and the two uraei are filled by an *ankh* and an *udjat* on each side. From the border hang rows of pendants shaped like lotus and papyrus blooms and buds, and roundels, an arrangement similar to border patterns used in contemporary paintings.

49 PECTORAL

Gold, cornelian (or rock crystal set in red cement), glass and greyish stone. Height 12.8 cm.; width 18.2 cm. Found in Tutankhamūn's tomb. Carter, Cat. no. 261 N. Late Eighteenth Dynasty

An enclosed pectoral in an architectonic frame decorated with the common arrangement of coloured strips and a double cornice. The central motif is a large scarab with the disk of the sun over its head. The scarab is supported by the goddesses Isis and Nephthys seated on either side. Cartouches with the king's names are placed between the sun and the heads of the goddesses. Both the design and the technical execution are similar to those of the pectoral shown in plate 37.

50 PECTORAL SHAPED LIKE A FALCON
    Gold, lapis lazuli, turqoise, cornelian, obsidian (?) and glass. Height 11.7 cm.; width 12.6 cm. Found in Tutankhamūn's tomb. Carter, Cat. no. 267 M (1) Late Eighteenth Dynasty
    Horus, the falcon, with widespread wings carries the sun on its head and the hieroglyphs *shenu* and *ankh* in its claws. The head is of beaten gold inlaid with lapis lazuli in the traditional way; the sun and the round centres of the *shenu* are of cornelian. The bird's claws are gold with engraved details; the formalized plumage on the body and wings is cloisonné incrustation work.

51 PECTORAL OF OSIRIS

Gold, silver, cornelian (or rock crystal set in red cement) and glass. Height 15.5 cm.; width 20 cm. Found in Tutankhamūn's tomb. Carter, Cat. no. 261 O. Late Eighteenth Dynasty.

An enclosed pectoral in an architectural frame and a double cornice. The central motif is a small figure of Osiris wearing an *atef* crown, with features resembling those of Tutankhamūn. On each side stand the vulture goddess Nekhbet, protectress of Upper Egypt, and the snake goddess Wadjet, protectress of Lower Egypt, both with wings outstretched to protect him. The inscriptions on the upright tablets, however, refer to the goddesses Isis and Nephthys. The pectoral is executed in openwork with cloisonné incrustation.

52 NECKLACE (or BRACELET?)

Red and yellow gold and blue faience. Measurements not available. Found in Tutankhamūn's tomb. Carter, Cat. no. 256 A. Late Eighteenth Dynasty

This necklace (or bracelet?) consists of three rows of large lentil-shaped beads ending in the calyces of lotus blooms inlaid with turquoise coloured faience. The fastening is shaped like two uraei with sun disks on their heads. The same sort of necklace adorns Tutankhamūn's neck on his first golden coffin.

53 BRACELET

Gold, lapis lazuli, cornelian and turquoise. Length 15.5 cm.; width 4.6 cm. Found in Tutankhamūn's tomb. Carter, Cat. no. 256 YY. Late Eighteenth Dynasty

A bracelet of three large scarabs, set with lapis lazuli, alternating with three groups of uraei and the hieroglyph *nefer* in a *neb* basket, topped by the sun. They are fixed between two lots of six strings of tiny beads ending in a slip fastening decorated with an inlaid locust.

54 BRACELET

Gold, lapis lazuli, cornelian and turquoise. Diameter 54 mm. Found in Tutankhamūn's tomb. Carter, Cat. no. 269 N. Late Eighteenth Dynasty

A massive gold bracelet of two parts hinged together. The upper and wider of the two is decorated with a large scarab set in lapis lazuli. The edge is a raised border of rectangles of gold, lapis lazuli, turquoise and cornelian. The trapeze-shaped space on the hinge is inlaid with mandrake fruit in yellow quartz, and buds in cornelian, and completed with gold rosettes.

56 EAR-RINGS WITH PENDANTS

Gold, quartz, alabaster, coloured faience, and blue, white and green glass. Length 10.9 cm.; width 52 mm. Found in Tutankhamūn's tomb. Carter, Cat. no. 269 A (1). Late Eighteenth Dynasty

The ear-rings are fastened by bosses, decorated on the outside with portraits of the monarch covered by thin pieces of transparent quartz and framed by two uraei. The pendants are heart-shaped plaques representing ducks with spread wings, their rounded heads of blue glass. Fixed to a gold bar below the birds' tails are loose strings of very small cylindrical beads and ornaments in gold, ending in five uraei.

◀ **55 BRACELET**

Gold, lapis lazuli, alabaster and turquoise coloured glass. Length of the whole bracelet 15.8 cm.; width 35 mm; height of the scarab 66 mm. Found in Tutankhamūn's tomb. Carter, Cat. no. 269 G. Late Eighteenth Dynasty

The bracelet consists of ten strings of elongated and spherical beads threaded through narrow spacers and ending in a straight fastening in which a large lapis lazuli scarab has been inserted; the *neb* basket below it is of turquoise blue glass. Its front legs hold a cartouche bearing Tutankhamūn's first name, Nebkheperurē.

57 EAR-RINGS WITH PENDANTS

Gold, cornelian, quartz, alabaster, coloured glass and faience. Length 10.9 cm.; width 52 mm. Found in Tutankhamūn's tomb. Carter, Cat. no. 269 A (3). Late Eighteenth Dynasty

The ear-rings are held in place by bosses, with the king's portrait between two uraei on the outer sides. The pendants are gold rings with outer rings of lentil-shaped beads, framing tiny cornelian statuettes of the young monarch standing on a *neb* basket between two uraei. A hawk with spread wings hides the string by which the pendant is attached to the boss. Six strings of round beads, spaced by granulated gold rings, and finished with large heart-shaped beads, hang from the rings.

58 EAR-RINGS

Gold, cornelian and coloured glass. Length 70 mm. Found in Tutankhamūn's tomb. Carter, Cat. no. 269 A (5). Late Eighteenth Dynasty

The large boss ear-rings have cornelian centres framed by granules of gold and three rings inlaid in dark blue and turquoise blue glass and cornelian. Two uraei with cornelian suns on their heads are attached to each ear-ring.

59 EAR-RINGS

Gold, resin and blue faience. Length 10 cm; diameter 55 mm. Found in Tutankhamūn's tomb. Carter, Cat. no. 269 A (2). Late Eighteenth Dynasty

The bosses are decorated with flowers with petals of red gold and the centres of yellow gold. The pendants are attached to the shanks of the ear-rings by semicircular flat links with granulated decorations. The body of the ear-rings are formed by round beads of red gold with granulated ornament in yellow gold, and six beads of reddish brown resin, threaded on a ring and separated from each other by flat rings of blue faience. A flat piece of curved gold, with a spiral design, fixed below the central lower bead, holds seven strings of blue and gold beads ending in drop beads of red gold and formalized flowers in yellow gold.

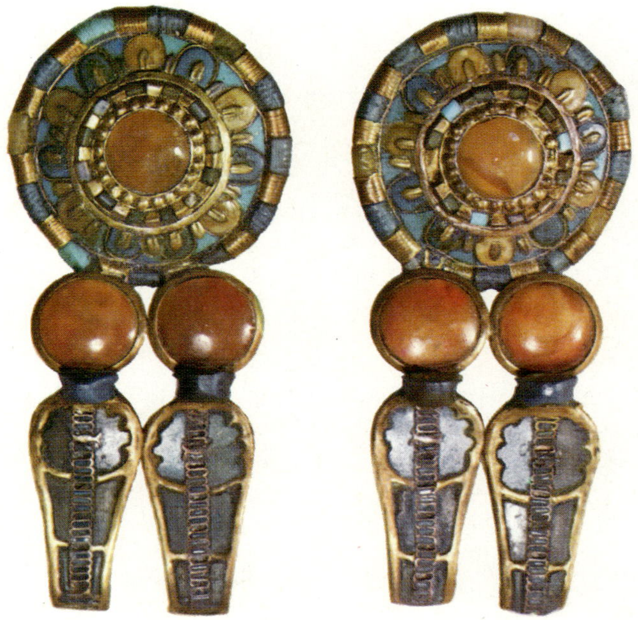

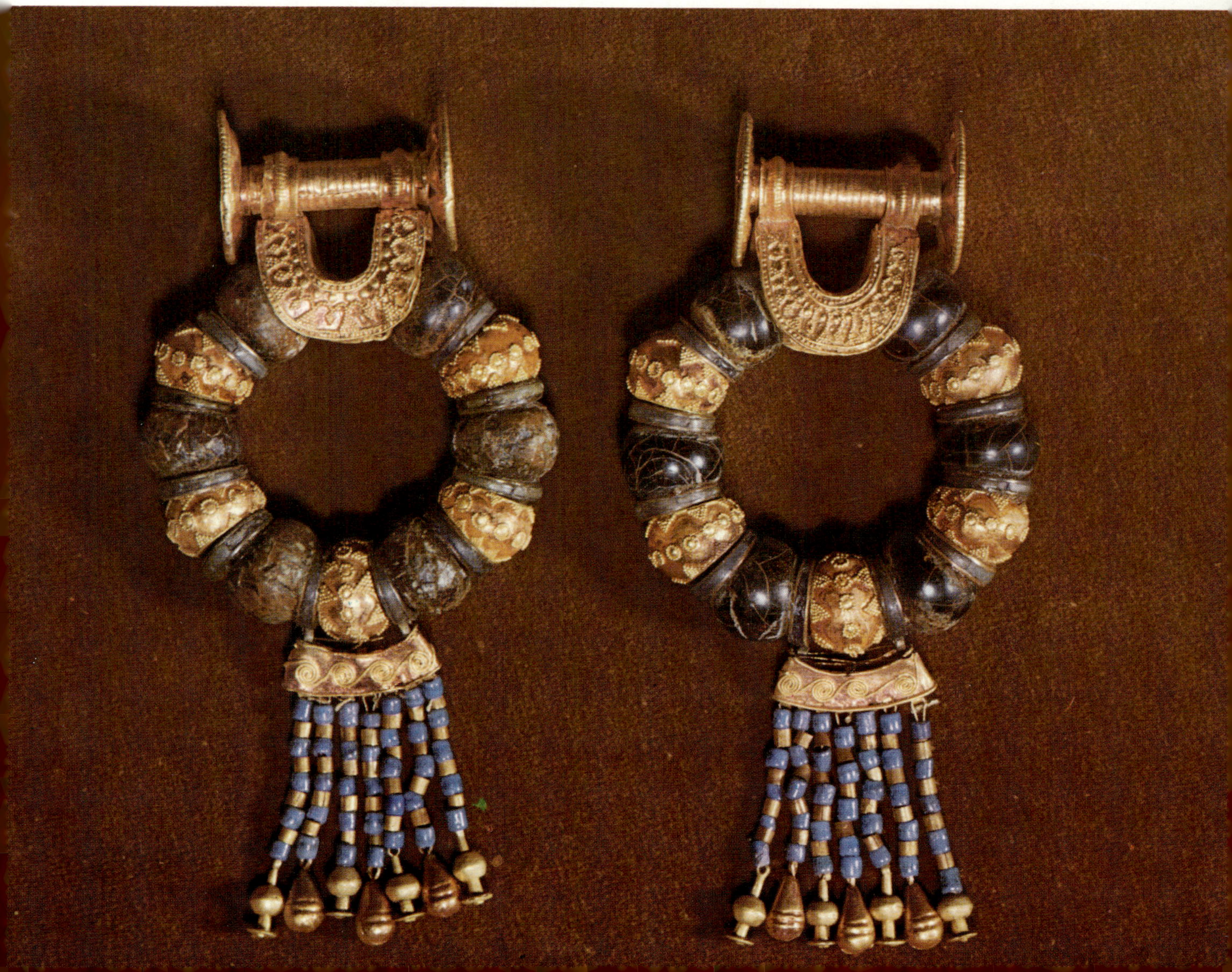

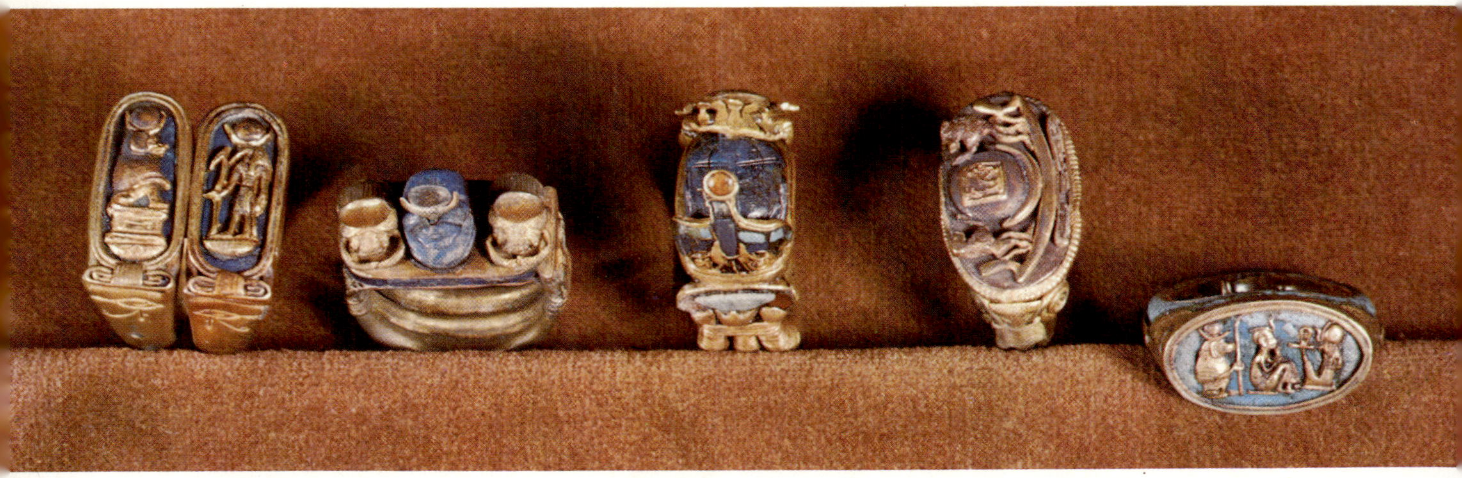

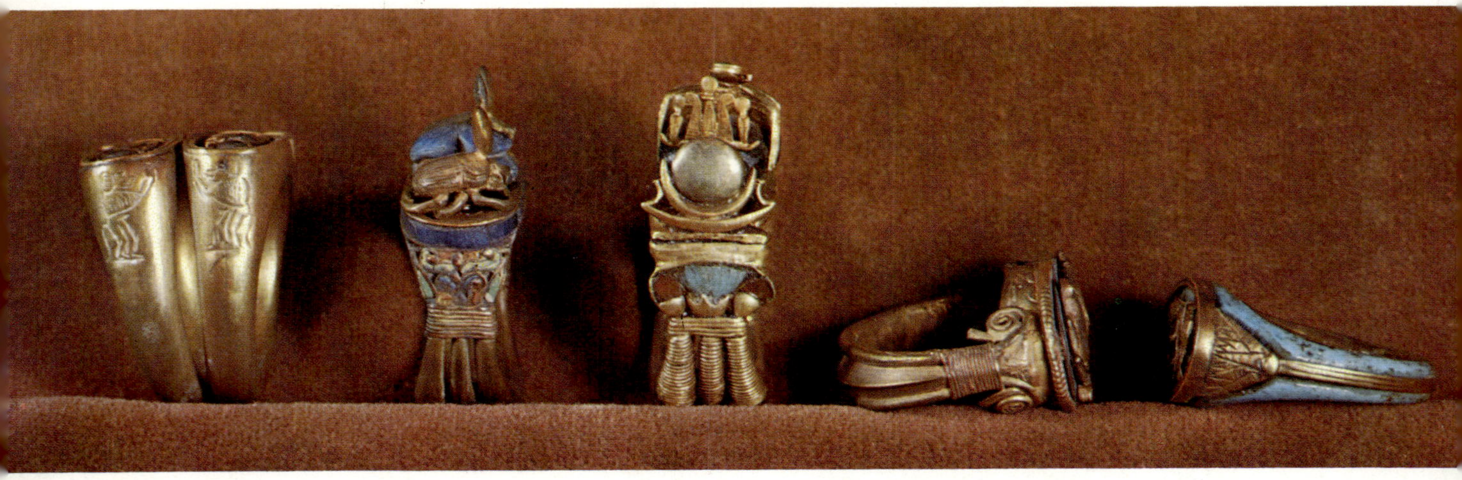

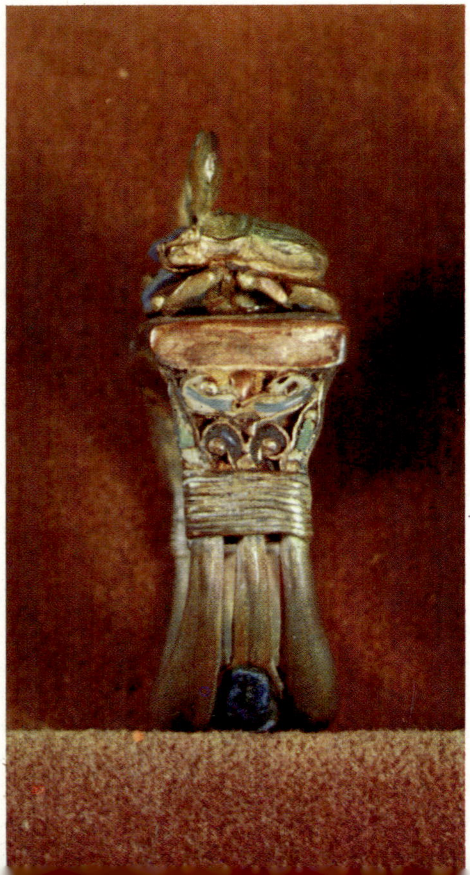

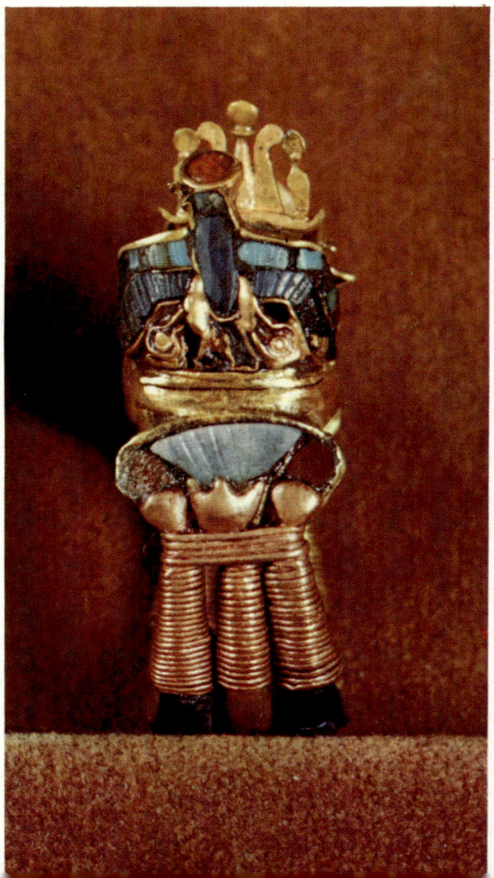

◀ **60a** RING

Gold. Diameter 18 mm.; bezel 18 × 15 mm. Found in Tutankhamūn's tomb. Carter, Cat. no. 44C. Late Eighteenth Dynasty

A massive gold ring decorated with a double cartouche showing in relief the god, Thoth, once as an ape and once as a man with an ibis head. Beneath the cartouches the *udjat* eye is carved on the ring.

◀ **60b** RING

Gold and blue glass. Inner diameter 21 mm.; width of the ring 11 mm. Found in Tutankhamūn's tomb. Carter, Cat. no. 44 D. Late Eighteenth Dynasty

A small cartouche fixed on the top of this triple ring supports three scarabs with the disk of the sun on their heads.

◀ **60c** RING

Gold and dark blue, turquoise and red glass. Inner diameter 20 mm.; width of the ring at the broadest point, 14 mm. Found in Tutankhamūn's tomb. Carter, Cat. no. 44 I. Late Eighteenth Dynasty

An unusually elaborate ring formed by three bands engraved crosswise and finished off with oval plaques bearing papyrus blooms and buds in turquoise blue and red glass. Between the plaques is an oval bezel with a blue scarab between a gold boat bearing a sun on one side and a hawk with spread wings on the other.

◀ **60d** RING

Gold. Inner diameter 22 mm.; width of the ring at the broadest point 7 mm. Found in Tutankhamūn's tomb. Carter, Cat. no. 44 E. Late Eighteenth Dynasty

The ring is in three parts, and is finished off by a papyrus bloom between two spiral scrolls. The oval bezel is carved in relief with a boat bearing a crescent moon and a sun, between two adoring apes.

◀ **60e** RING

Gold and turquoise glass. Inner diameter 19 mm. Found in Tutankhamūn's tomb. Carter, Cat. No 44 F. Late Eighteenth Dynasty

The gold band of the ring is decorated with a lotus stem ending in a flower, and is inlaid with turquoise blue glass. The oval bezel has a gold relief design on a turquoise blue background, showing the king seated between Horus and Thoth as an ape.

◀ **61 - 63** RINGS (Another views and details of the rings shown in plate 60)

◀ **64 GOLD APPLIQUÉ ELEMENT**
Red and yellow gold. Height 62 mm.; width 85 mm. Found in Tutankhamūn's tomb. Carter, Cat. no. 44 A. Late Eighteenth Dynasty

A gold appliqué element or plaque, one of four similar pieces, in openwork design of reddish gold, partly engraved and partly decorated with granulation in yellow gold. The scene shows the young pharaoh returning from a military campaign on a two-wheeled chariot drawn by two elaborately caparisoned horses. A group of prisoners precede the chariot, and behind stands a winged cobra, the goddess Wadjet, holding the king's cartouche between her wings. The vulture goddess Nekhbet soars above. In the bottom panel is a scene of the 'uniting of the two lands', between the flower symbols of Upper and Lower Egypt, the lily and the papyrus. This illustration of a triumphal return from war is unlikely to refer to an actual event.

65 GOLD APPLIQUÉ ELEMENT
Red and yellow gold. Measurements as for plate 64. Found in Tutankhamūn's tomb. Carter, Cat. no. 44 A. Late Eighteenth Dynasty

The technique is the same as in the previous example. The scene in the central panel represents a pavilion with pillars formed by bunches of lotus blooms supporting lily and papyrus blooms and these, in turn, carry a triple cornice surmounted by a row of uraei. In the pavilion Tutankhamūn is seated and Ankhesenamūn is offering him a bunch of papyrus blooms. In the trapeze-shaped panels at either side are two recumbent sphinxes; the one on the left has a human head, the one on the right a lion's. Both are holding *neb* baskets with figures of the goddess of truth, Maat. Beyond the sphinxes rises the vulture goddess Nekhbet with a feather fan in her claws. In the segmental panel below the pavilion are defeated enemies, and above the pavilion is a winged sun-disk.

66 GOLDEN THRONE OF TUTANKHAMŪN
Wood covered with gold leaf, inlaid with gold and silver, coloured glass, faience and alabaster. Height 104 cm.; depth 64.5 cm.; width 53 cm. Found in Tutankhamūn's tomb. Carter, Cat. no. 91. Late Eighteenth Dynasty

The feet of the throne are shaped like lions' paws, and the front legs end in lions' heads at the level of the seat. The arms are decorated with winged cobras wearing the double crown of Upper and Lower Egypt and holding between their wings cartouches with the royal names. The reverse side of the back shows a papyrus thicket with two water birds in flight in beaten gold. Between the upright supports there are uraei with sun-disks on their heads and above them is a cornice of lotus blooms and buds. Robbers seem to have broken and made off with the gilt braces from between the legs of the throne.

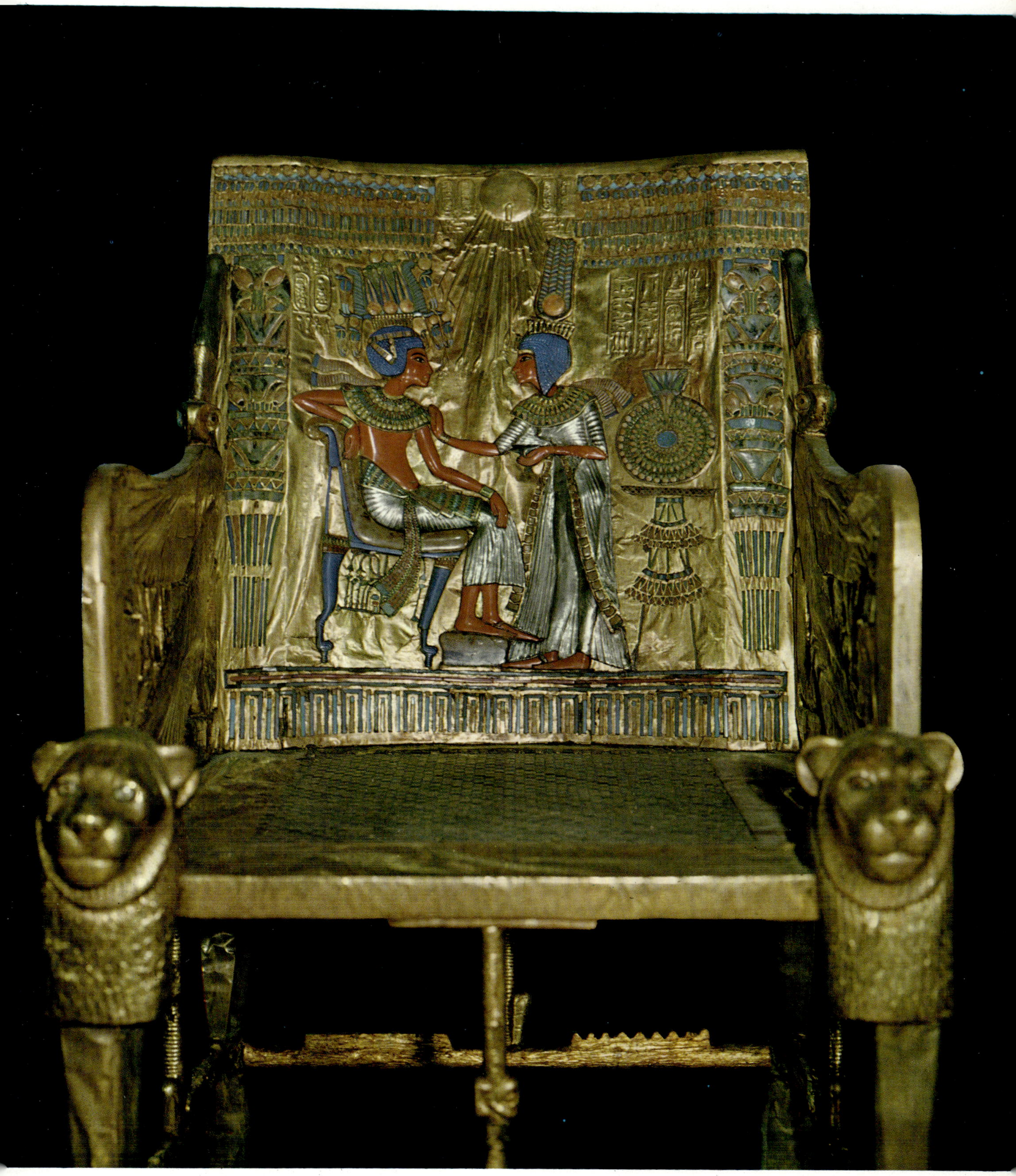

67 BACK OF TUTANKHAMŪN'S THRONE (Detail of plate 66)

The scene on the back of the throne shows Tutankhamūn and his wife, Ankhesenamūn, in an interior indicated by an architectural base, plant stems and flower pilasters at the sides, and a broad quadruple cornice above interrupted in the centre by a sun with rays ending in hands. The young king is sitting informally on his throne on the left, his right arm resting on back of the throne. The queen stands in front of him with a bowl of perfumed unguent in her left arm while her right hand is touching the king's shoulder. On a small table behind her there is a necklace of many rows of beads. The rich dress and elaborate crowns they are wearing are somewhat at variance with the informality of the scene. The garments are executed in silver, the unclothed parts of their bodies in reddish brown glass, the wigs are inlaid in bright blue faience, and coloured glass and alabaster have been used for the details of the jewellery.

68 NECKLACE

Gold and cornelian. Height 33 cm.; width 36 cm. Found at Tell Basta (Zagazig) in 1907. Cat. Gén. 53184. Nineteenth Dynasty

This necklace is made up of nineteen rows of beads held together by tiny spacers, the first and last being single and the others triple. The small round beads are gold, while the lentil-shaped beads are partly gold, partly cornelian, as are the pendants shaped like Egyptian cornflowers.

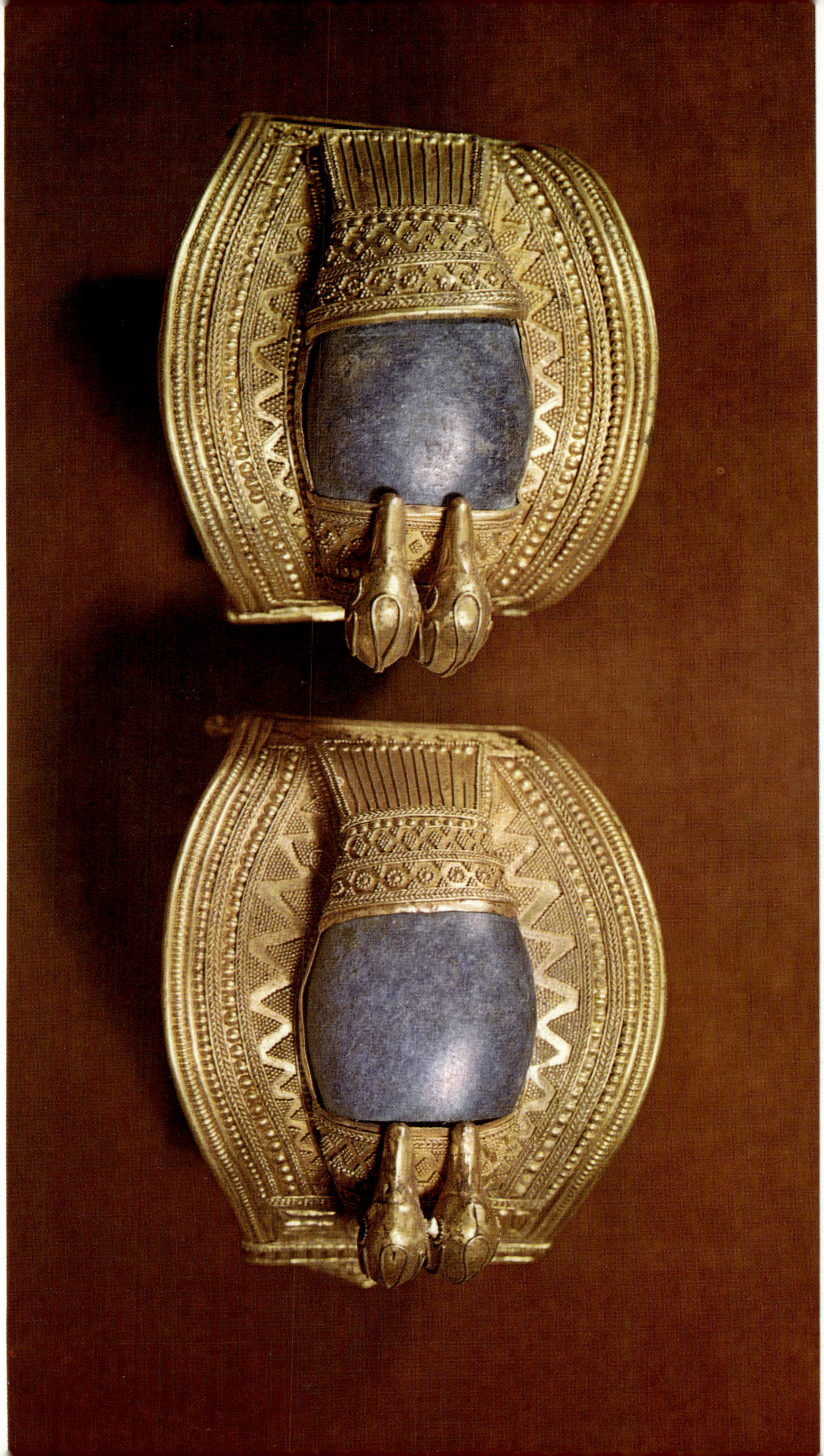

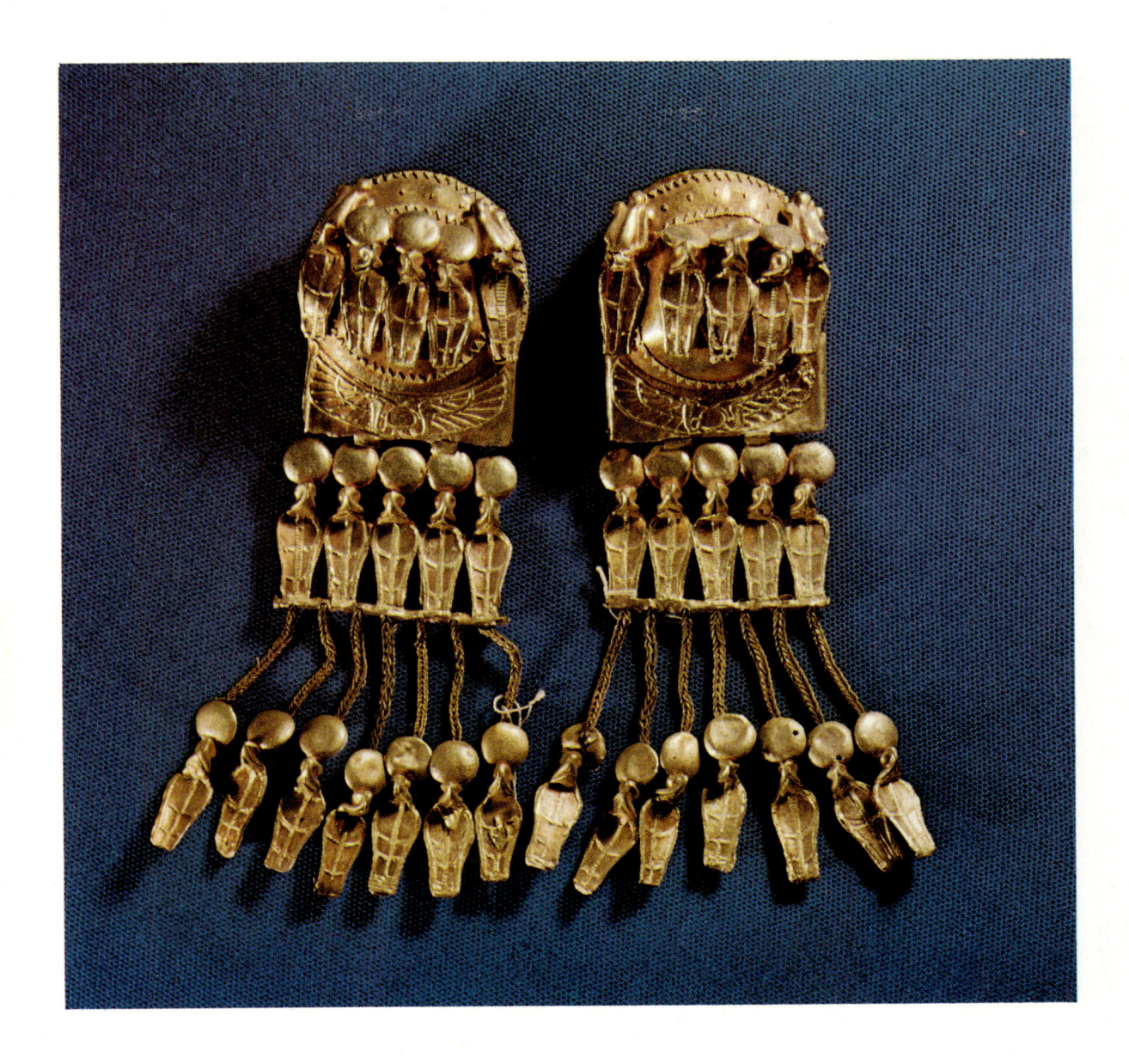

70 EAR-RINGS OF RAMESSES XI
   Red gold. Length 16 cm.; width 53 mm. Found at Abydos. Cat. Gén. 52323—4. Twentieth Dynasty
   These ear-rings are in three parts, one above the other: a large boss with a design of five uraei with the disk of the sun and an *atef* crown on each head and a winged sun below; another row of five uraei standing on a bar; and, suspended from the bar, seven short chains also ending in uraei. The ear-rings are of reddish beaten gold with the details in fine strips of granulation.

◀ **69 BRACELETS OF RAMESSES II**
   Gold and lapis lazuli. Diameter 56 mm.; width at the broadest point 59 mm. Found at Tell Basta (Zagazig). Cat Gén. 52575—6. Nineteenth Dynasty
   This pair of massive gold bracelets made in two parts and hinged, in one case with a sliding pin, are decorated, on the broader upper half with two goose heads on a single body, inlaid in lapis lazuli. The upper and lower part of the body and the background are in gold with granulated decoration; the heads and tails have details in soldered gold wire. There are several rows of alternate cable and tress pattern round the edge. By the hinges there are cartouches with the king's name. The lower half is marked with horizontal grooves.

71a RING
Gold and green schist. Length of the bezel 19 mm. Cat. Gén. 52192. New Kingdom
The scarab carved in green schist is set in a gold frame fixed to the band of the ring by means of pins.

71b RING
Gold and blue faience. Diameter 20 mm. Cat. Gén. 52215. New Kingdom
The bezel is flat on both sides and the ornament is carved in hollow relief. It is attached to the band by means of gold wire threaded through the crown and through holes in the flattened ends of the band.

71c RING
Gold and cornelian. Diameter 25 mm. (Formerly in the Huber collection). Cat Gén. 52198. Eighteenth Dynasty
The bezel in is the form of the *udjat* eye, carved in cornelian and held in place by a gold wire passing through it and twisted round the band of the ring. On the reverse of the bezel is the cartouche of Thutmose IV.

71d RING
Gold and steatite. Diameter 23 mm. (Formerly in the Huber collection). Cat. Gén. 52206. New Kingdom
The pin, which goes through the body of the scarab, fits into holes in each end of the flattened band of the ring; the ends of the pin have been hammered so that they cannot slip out.

72 PECTORAL

Gilt wood, resin, cornelian and glass. Height 11 cm.; width 14 cm. Found at Qurna in 1896. Cat. Gén. 53201. New Kingdom

An enclosed pectoral in an architectonic frame with the traditional pattern and a double cornice. A large scarab of chestnut-coloured resin is set in the centre with, on the right, the hieroglyph *tit* carved in cornelian and, on the left, *djed* in cornelian and turquoise and dark blue glass.

73 PECTORAL (Reverse of the pectoral in plate 72)

The central features are the underside of the scarab, with an inscription, and on either side the goddesses Isis and Nephthys kneeling on the hieroglyph for gold. The text of the inscription concerns the owner of the pectoral, the scribe and local ruler Ibay. (The transcription in Cat. Gén. is incorrect.) The words are not taken from spell 30 B of the 'Book of the Dead' as is usual for 'heart' scarabs.

74 PECTORAL OF KING PSIBKHENNĒ (PSUSENNES)

Gold and semi-precious stones. Height 12 cm.; width 12 cm. Found in the royal necropolis at Tanis in 1940. Montet, Tanis no. 506. Twenty-first Dynasty

An enclosed pectoral in the usual architectonic frame. The centre of the composition is a scarab of ivory or imitation ivory, in a poor state of preservation. A small *djed* pillar stands below the scarab, and on either side cartouches with the king's names and the hieroglyph for universal rule, *shenu*. This central motif is framed by the open wings of the goddesses Isis and Nephthys, one on either side. Over the raised arm of each is an *udjat* eye with an uraeus. A hinge joins a pendant panel to the lower border. The panel shows a calyx which resembles a *wesekh* collar counterpoise in shape, with on each side an uraeus and a boat bearing the pharaoh facing on the left the god Osiris and on the right a large heron. The pectoral is in openwork with cloisonné incrustation.

75 PECTORAL OF KING PSIBKHENNĒ (PSUSENNES)

Gold, semi-precious stones and coloured pebbles. Height 11 cm. Found in the royal necropolis at Tanis in 1940. Montet, Tanis no. 509. Twenty-first Dynasty

An open pectoral in the form of a winged scarab, which is cut from a greenish-blue pebble, well ground and polished. The wings are divided horizontally by strips of gold and the spaces inlaid with oblong stones of light and dark greens and pinks. Below the scarab is *shenu* (universal rule), and above it between the wings is the cartouche of Psusennes, first prophet of Amūn. A text from spell 126 of the 'Book of the Dead' is inscribed on the reverse of the scarab.

76 PECTORAL OF KING HEKAKHEPERRĒ SHESHONQ

Gold, lapis lazuli, cornelian and glass. Width 78 mm. Found in the royal necropolis at Tanis in 1940. Montet, Tanis no. 219. Twenty-second Dynasty.

This framed enclosed pectoral has a lower border of gold zigzags on a blue ground representing water, an upper border of the hieroglyph *pet* (heaven) with a row of stars, and the stems of the symbolical flowers of Upper and Lower Egypt at the sides (lily and papyrus). A gold boat bears a lapis lazuli sun-disk with the figure of the god Amon-Rē-Harakhty in relief, with the goddess of right and justice, Maat, standing in front of him. There is a winged goddess on either side of the sun, perhaps Isis on the left and Maat on the right. In the lower corners of the pectoral are two plaques inscribed with a prayer to the god to protect king Sheshonq. Pendants shaped like lotus buds and blooms hang from the lower edge of the pectoral and a pair of falcons with double crowns on their heads are perched on the top corners.

77a PENDANT

Gold. Height 109 mm. Found in the royal necropolis at Tanis in 1940. Montet, Tanis no. 726. Twenty-first Dynasty

A pendant in the shape of the goddess Isis with the sun-disk on her head between her horns. An uraeus is rearing up on her forehead. The details are chased. The chain, of the 'colonne doublée' type, 80 cm. long, is attached to a ring on the back of the sun-disk.

◀ **77b PENDANT**

Gold. Height 93 mm. Found in the royal necropolis at Tanis in 1940. Montet, Tanis no. 727. Twenty-first Dynasty

A pendant possibly in the shape of the goddess Bastet with a lion's head, and the disk of the sun with an uraeus in front and a ring for a chain at the back. The details are engraved.

◀ **77c PENDANT**

Gold. Height 72 mm. Found in the royal necropolis at Tanis in 1940. Montet, Tanis no. 728. Twenty-first Dynasty

A pendant similar to the previous one, possibly in the form of the goddess Bastet with a lion's head. The details are engraved.

78 BRACELET OF KING PSIBKHENNĒ (PSUSENNES)

Gold and lapis lazuli. Length *c.* 21 cm.; width 35 mm. Found in the royal necropolis at Tanis in 1940. Montet, Tanis no. 598—9. Twenty-first Dynasty

One of a pair of bracelets thought, because of the position in which they were found, to be intended to be worn on the leg, at the knee. They were part of a set, the other pair which is meant for the ankle is so small that it would hardly fit the most slender woman. The knee bracelets are also very small. It is possible that the smaller pair were really arm bracelets, and the larger pair either bracelets or anklets.

The one shown in the plate is composed of four oblong gold plaques with, on all sides, hinges engraved with cartouches containing the complete set of titles given to the king. They are linked together by separate segmental strips of gold and lapis lazuli. The whole bracelet is edged with a string of cylindrical beads.

79 BRACELET OF KING HEKAKHEPERRE SHESHONQ

Gold and semi-precious stones. Height 47 mm.; diameter 65 mm. Found in the royal necropolis at Tanis in 1940. Montet, Tanis no. 226—7. Twenty-second Dynasty

One of a pair of bracelets found in the tomb of king Sheshonq. They are both made of two segments of unequal size hinged together with a sliding pin. The central motif is a square set with a *udjat* eye on a *neb* basket. The rest of the design is composed of gold strips alternating with blue, and the edging is of the typical alternate coloured rectangles.

80 RING

Gold and semi-precious stones, or glass. Height 18 mm. Found in the royal necropolis at Tanis in 1940. Montet, Tanis no. 562. Twenty-first Dynasty

A broad ring ornamente with cloisonné incrustation, and divided into six sections by strips of alternate inlaid coloured rectangles. Two sections contain a royal cartouche while the others are filled with a diamond and triangle pattern.

81 SHIELDS FOR THE TOES OF THE MUMMY

Gold. Height 25—50 mm. Found in the tomb of king Psibkhennē (Psusennes) at Tanis. Montet, Tanis nos. 602—621. Cat. Gén. nos. 85836—40. Twenty-first Dynasty

These shields for the toes of the king's mummy are of beaten gold, adorned with simple rings. The whole set for the fingers and toes consists of twenty shields.

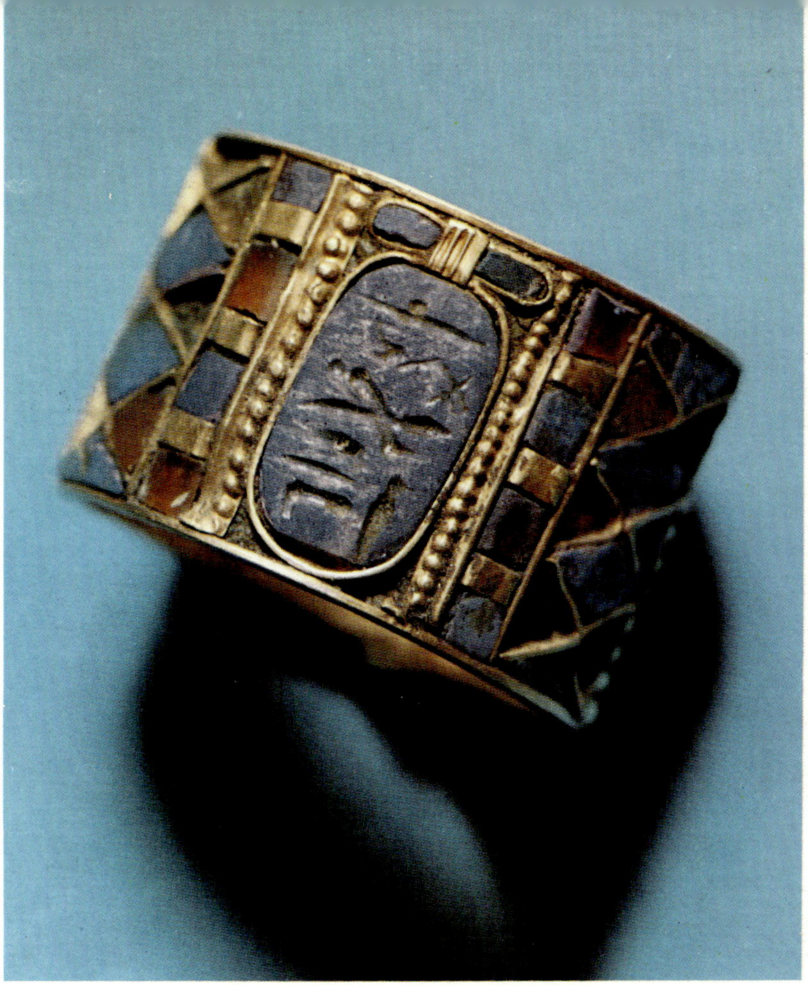

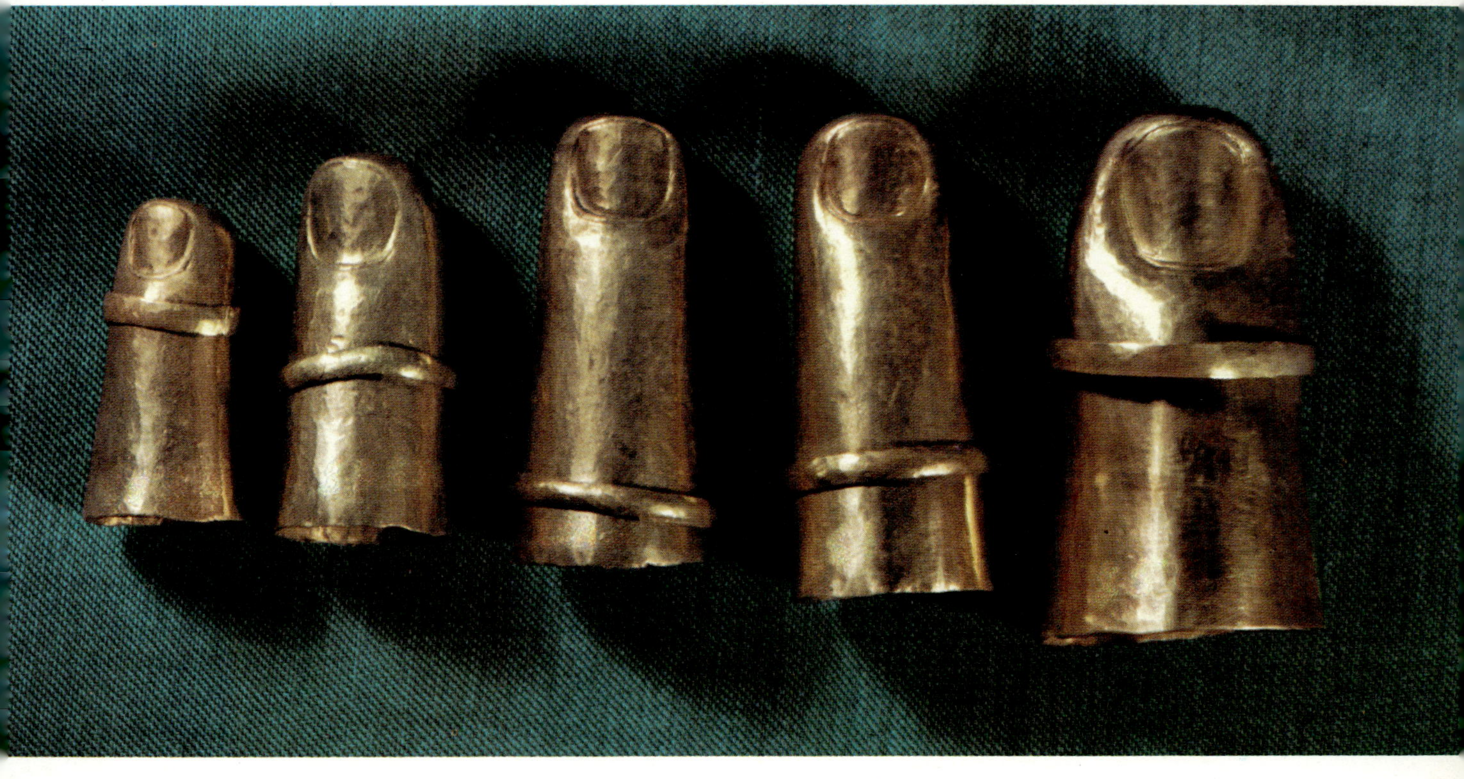

82 PLATE FOR COVERING THE ABDOMINAL INCISION IN THE MUMMY
Gold. 165 × 98 mm. Found in the coffin of king Psibkhennē (Psusennes) in 1940. Montet, Tanis, no. 527. Twenty-first Dynasty

The beaten gold plate is decorated with a relief design showing the four sons of Horus lifting the *udjat* eye. Imset and Hapy are on the left, and Duamutef and Quebehsenuf on the right. Above are their names in oblong frames, and the king's cartouche. The plate was meant to cover and protect the abdominal incision through which the entrails of the dead person were removed before mummification.

83 BRACELET OF PINEDJEM
Gold, lapis lazuli and cornelian. Outer diameter 68 mm.; thickness 8 mm. Found in the tomb of the high priest Pinedjem in 1886. Cat. Gén. 52089. Twenty-first Dynasty

This massive bracelet, horse-shoe shaped in cross-section and flat on the inside, is made in two sections joined at one end by a lapis lazuli bead and at the other by a fastening with a sliding pin. It is decorated with cloisonné incrustation, and the motifs are separated by broad rings of gold. Two gold chains and two strings of cylindrical beads, ending in six-petalled calyces, hang from it.

84a RING
Gold, lapis lazuli and cornelian. Width 20 mm. Found at Abusīr in 1888. Cat. Gén. 52165. Late Dynastic Period

This triple ring of gold is divided into three separate parts, each of which has an oval stone set in a granulated gold frame.

84b RING
Gold and semi-precious stones. Width, measured through the stones, 22 mm. Found at Saqqāra in 1893. Cat. Gén. 52167. Late Dynastic Period

A massive ring with incrustation ornament; in the centre there are three oval stones set one above the other, with lotus blooms at the sides. The incrustation is badly damaged, although the cornelian in the centre has survived quite well.

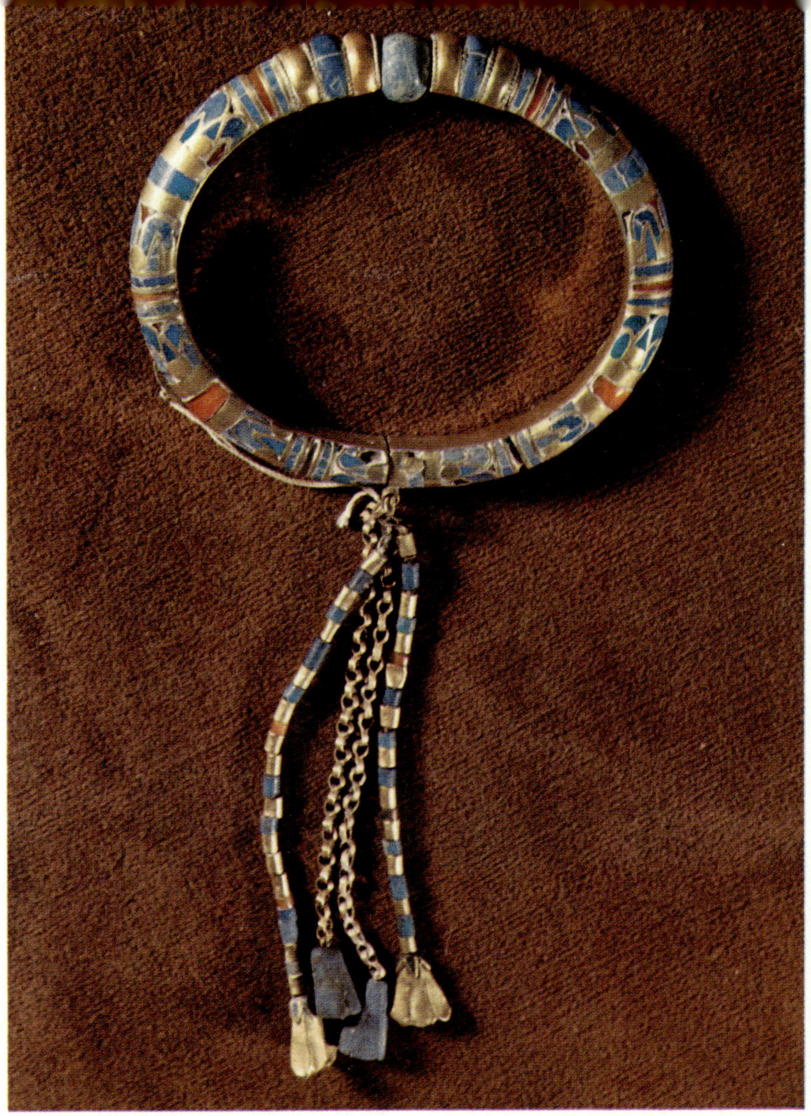

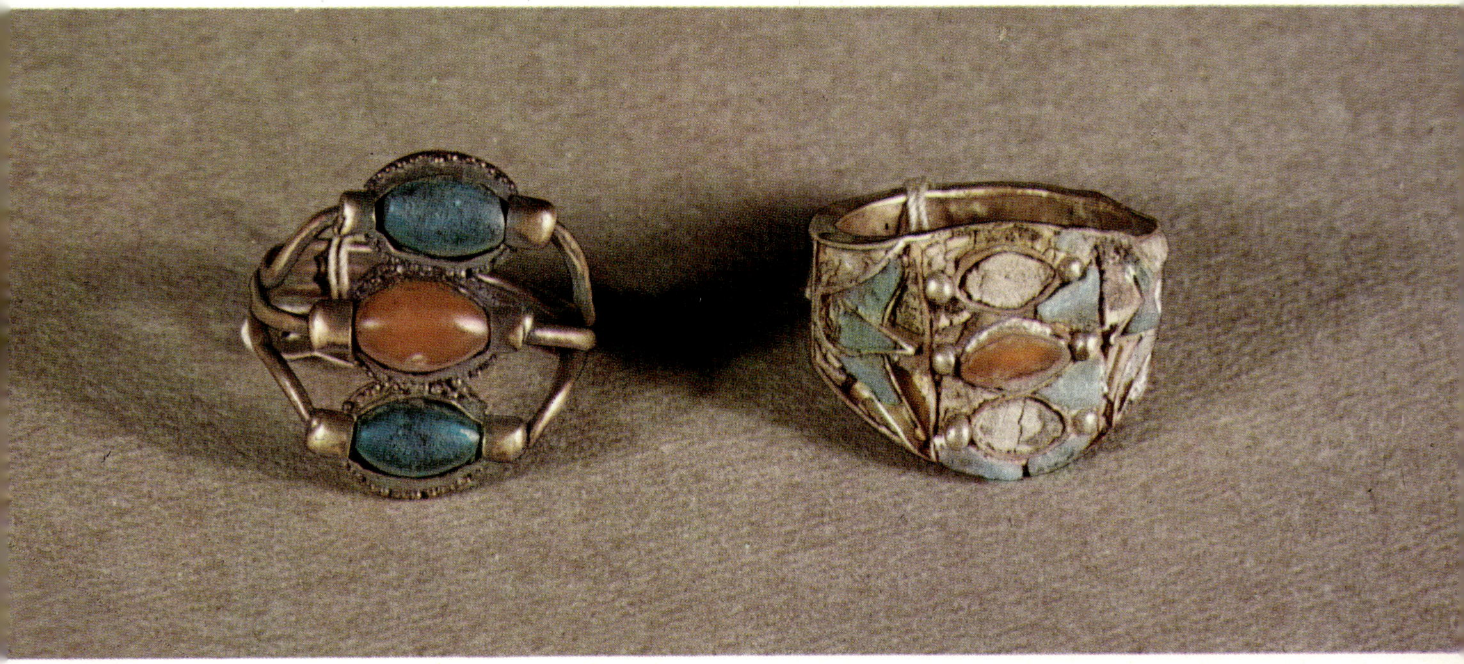

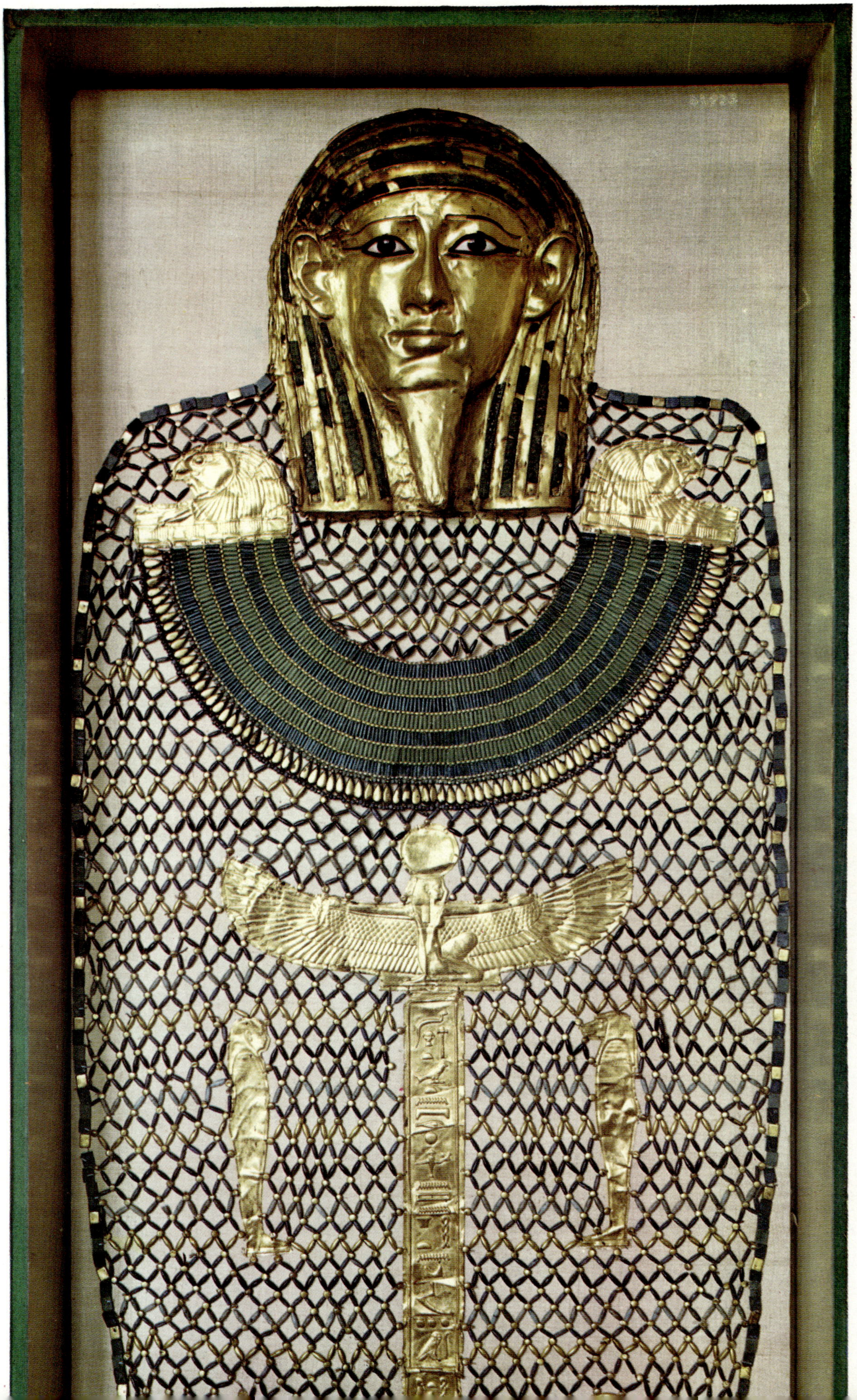

86 BRACELET

    Gold. Distance from one head to the other 14.5 cm.; length of the spiral 60 mm.; width of the band 7 mm. Found in the eastern delta. Cat. Gén. 52123. Roman period, first century A.D.

    A bracelet shaped like a two-headed snake. The spirally twisted band is of beaten gold with engraved details on the moulded heads. The heads are made of two pieces of gold leaf, the larger forming the upper side, and the gaps filled with plaster.

◀ **85 BEAD SHROUD OF A MUMMY**

    Gold, lapis lazuli, green felspar, faience and obsidian. Height 145 cm.; width 46 cm. Reconstructed from separate pieces found in the tomb of Tjanenhebu at Saqqāra. Cat. Gén. 53668. Twenty-sixth Dynasty

    The mummy's apparel consists of a gold mask inlaid with felspar, obsidian and lapis lazuli; a *wesekh* collar with beads of lapis lazuli, felspar and gold, and drop pendants and a hawk's head fastening; and a shroud of beaded mesh. This mesh is made of elongated beads of gold, lapis lazuli and green felspar, and spherical gold beads. Down the middle runs a gold band with a prayer in hieroglyphs to the goddess Nut, whose kneeling figure with widespread wings ends the band at the top. The sons of Horus are arranged on both sides.

87 BRACELET

Gold and beryls. Length of the spiral 76 mm.; width of the band 7 mm. Found at Sa el-Hagar (Sais) in 1906. Cat. Gén. 52114. Roman period, first century A.D.

A massive gold snake bracelet with the details on the head and tail chased; the eyes and the top of the head are inlaid with beryls.

88 RING

Gold. Diameter 21 mm.; width of the bezel 6 mm. Bought in 1893. Cat. Gén. 52296. Hellenistic period

A massive gold ring with a bezel in relief, representing the bust of Serapis.

89a BRACELET

Gold. and agate. Longer diameter 65 mm.; thickness 8 mm.; bezel 25 × 22 mm. Found at Kom Abu Billo in 1903. Cat. Gén. 52101. Roman period, third century A.D.

Three thick gold wires are twisted in a spiral and fixed in hollow cylinders fitted with rings. The crown has a convex segmented edge and an oval agate in the centre; it is also fitted with rings and held in place with pins, one fixed and one sliding. The crown is of gold leaf filled with plaster.

89b BRACELET

Gold and agate. Longer diameter 80 mm.; thickness 10 mm.; bezel 36 × 35 mm. Found at Zagazig (Bubastis) in 1881. Cat. Gén. 52099. Roman period, third century A.D.

The bracelet is formed by three hollow gold tubes twisted into a spiral ending in hollow cylinders with rings and pins holding the large oval crown in place. The crown is slightly conical in shape and an agate is set in the centre. The crown and the tubes are filled with plaster.

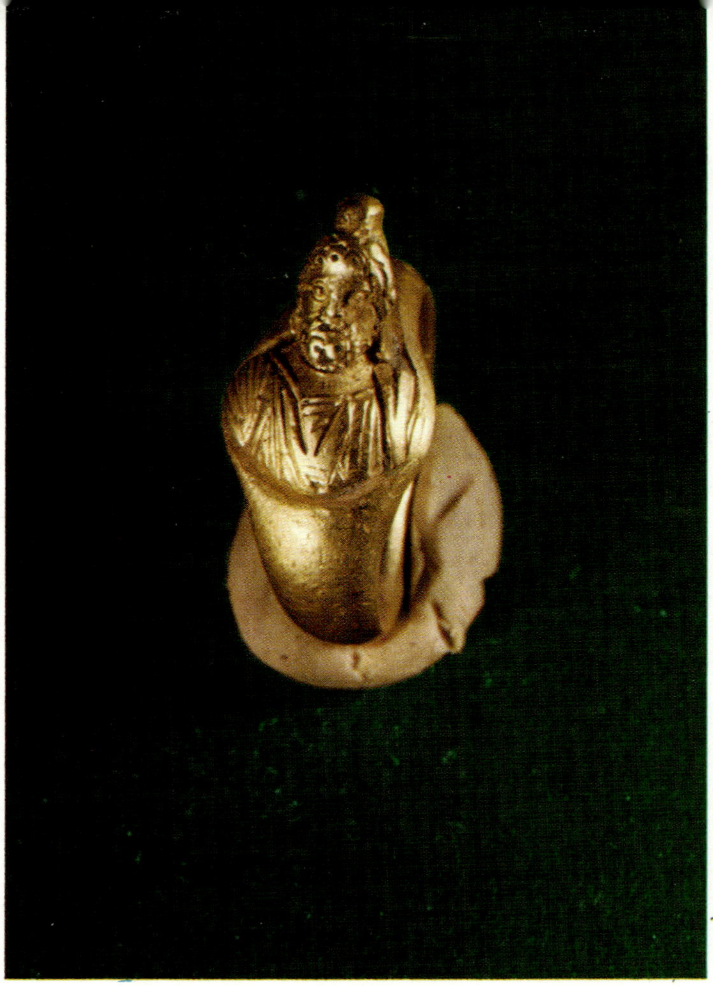

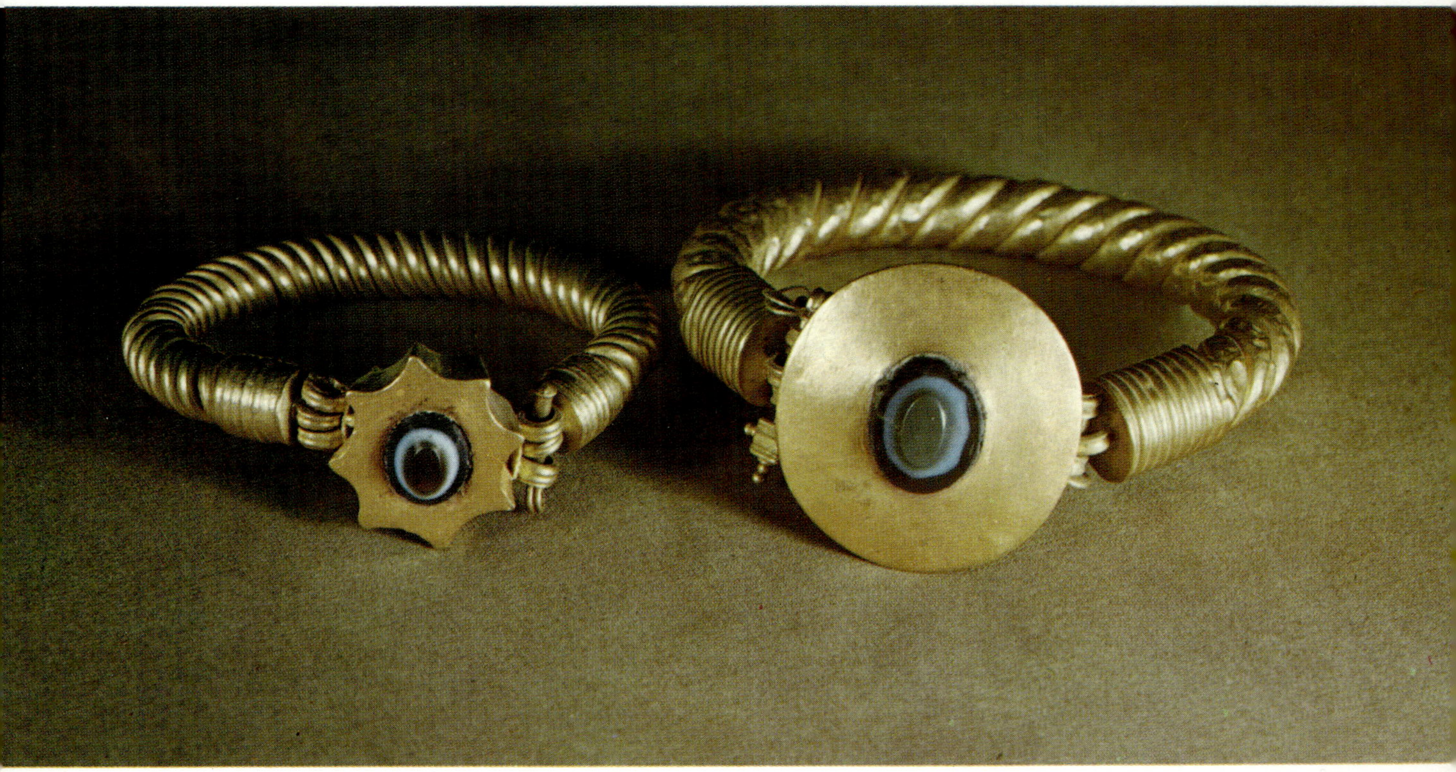

90a RING

Gold and green jasper. Inner diameter 18 mm., length of the bezel 19 mm. Found at Mit Rahîna (Memphis) in 1903. Cat. Gén. 52306. Hellenistic period

A ring of thin sheet gold beaten to a rounded shape and fastened inside by a strip of gold soldered on. The ground stone is shaped like an olive.

90b RING

Gold and green jasper. Diameter 20 mm.; bezel 16 × 11 mm. Acquired by exchange in 1894. Cat. Gén. 52293. Hellenistic period

The ring is formed by two thick pieces of gold wire joined in a sailor's knot with the ends separated towards the crown. The stone has been cut to a semi-cylindrical shape and set in a decorative surround of astragal, egg and dart and ovular granulation.

90c RING

Gold and lapis lazuli. Diameter 26 mm.; length of the bezel 19 mm. Cat. Gén. 52304. Hellenistic period

A spiral ring ending in two goats' heads to which a moveable bezel is fixed with pins. The frame of the bezel is broad and raised. On the reverse are the gods Serapis, Aesculapius and Hygieia (?).

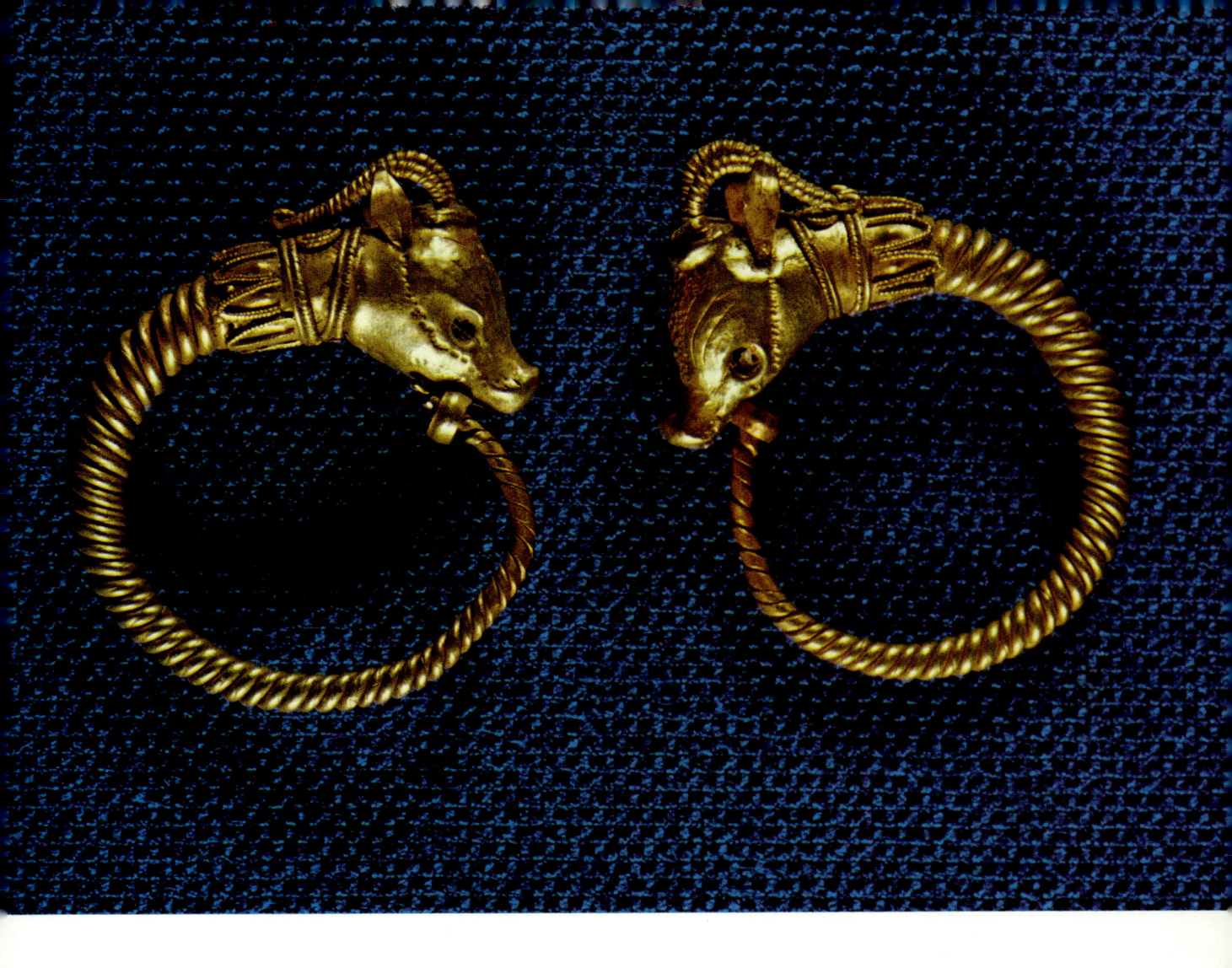

91 EAR-RINGS

   Gold. Diameter 32 mm. (Formerly in the Huber collection). Cat. Gén. 52522–3. Hellenistic period, third century B.C.
   The hoops of spirally twisted gold wire end in moulded antelope heads with engraved detail. Their pointed collars are decorated with granulation.

92 EAR-RINGS

Gold. Diameter 29 and 30 mm. Found at Abydos in 1881. Cat. Gén. 52528–9. Hellenistic period, third century B.C.

These rings are executed in the same way as the previous pair. The hoops end in bulls' heads decorated with tress ornament soldered on.

93 EAR-RINGS

Gold. Length 30 mm.; width 20 mm. Found at Mit Rahîna (Memphis). Cat. Gén. 52441—2. Roman period
The wires by which the ear-rings are fixed pass through the sickle-shaped bodies. From the centre hang cylindrical ornaments with rows of beaten beads in relief, ending in a lentil-shape. The ear-rings are made of thin gold leaf with a solid filling.

94 EAR-RING

Gold. Diameter 23 mm.; height of the basket 13 mm. (Formerly in the Huber collection). Cat. Gén. 52523. Byzantine period

This ear-ring shaped like a small round basket is made of three separate pieces joined together by a soldered cable decoration with moulded beads at the narrowest points of contact. The basket is openwork, with holes shaped like a figure eight.

CHRONOLOGICAL TABLE

PREHISTORIC

date B.C.	period	culture	important jewellery found at
c. 5000	Neolithic		
c. 4000	Chalcolithic	Badarian	Badari
		Amratian	Naqāda
		Gerzean	

c. 3200 Union of Upper and Lower Egypt under one king

HISTORIC

date B.C.	dynasty	important jewellery found at
PROTODYNASTIC PERIOD		
c. 3200	First	Abydos — in the tomb of king Djer
c. 2900	Second	
OLD KINGDOM		
c. 2700	Third	Saqqāra — in the pyramid of king Sekhemket
c. 2615	Fourth	Gīza — belonging to queen Hetepheres and an unknown princess
c. 2500	Fifth and Sixth	
FIRST INTERMEDIATE PERIOD		
c. 2180	Seventh to mid-Eleventh	
MIDDLE KINGDOM		
c. 2080	late Eleventh	
c. 1990	Twelfth	el-Lisht — belonging to princess Senebtisi
		Dahshūr — belonging to princesses Khnumet and Mereret
		el-Lāhūn — belonging to princess Sithathoriunet
SECOND INTERMEDIATE PERIOD		
c. 1785	Thirteenth to Seventeenth	tombs of el-Asasif
NEW KINGDOM		
c. 1575	Eighteenth	Qurna — belonging to queen Ahhotpe
		Sheikh Abd el-Qurna — belonging to princesses Menwi, Merti and Menhet of the harem of Thutmose III
		Thebes — in the tomb of Tutankhamūn
c. 1304	Nineteenth and Twentieth	
LATE DYNASTIC PERIOD		
c. 1075	Twenty-first and Twenty-second	Tanis
c. 817	Twenty-third to Thirtieth	
332	GREEK PERIOD	
30-A.D. 395	ROMAN PERIOD	

LIST OF ILLUSTRATIONS

1 BRACELET. Gold, lapis lazuli and turquoise. Length 10.2 cm. Found at Umm el-Gaāb (Abydos) on the arm of a Thinite princess. First Dynasty

2 BRACELET. Gold and turquoise. Length 15.6 cm. Found at Umm el-Gaāb (Abydos) on the arm of the mummy of a Thinite princess. First Dynasty

3 BRACELET. Gold, amethyst and turquoise. Length 15 cm. Found at Umm el-Gaāb (Abydos) on the arm of the mummy of a Thinite princess. First Dynasty

4 BRACELET. Gold, lapis lazuli and turquoise. Length 13 cm. Found at Umm el-Gaāb (Abydos) on the arm of the mummy of a Thinite princess. First Dynasty

5 FILLET. Gold, copper and cornelian. Diameter 25 cm.; width of the band 38 mm. Found at Gīza, in the tomb of an unknown princess. Fourth Dynasty

6 NECKLACE. Gold. Length of each bead 27 mm.; length of the necklace c. 50 cm. Found at Gīza, in the tomb of an unknown princess. Fourth Dynasty

7 BUCKLE (Detail of plate 8)

8 BELT OF PRINCE PTAHSHEPSES. Gold, cornelian and blue and green faience. Length of buckle 10 cm.; width 45 mm.; length of belt 90 cm.; width 45 mm. Found at Saqqāra during excavation of the valley temple of the pyramid of Unis. Fifth Dynasty

9 PECTORAL OF SENWOSRET III. Gold, lapis lazuli, cornelian and turquoise. Height 61 mm.; width 85 mm. Found at Dahshūr, in the tomb of princess Mereret. Twelfth Dynasty

10 PECTORAL OF AMENEMHET III. Gold, lapis lazuli, cornelian and glazed material. Height 79 mm.; width 10.4 cm. Found at Dahshūr in the tomb of princess Mereret. Twelfth Dynasty

11 PECTORAL OF AMENEMHET III. Gold, lapis lazuli, cornelian and some unidentifiable substance. Height 47 mm.; width 82 mm. Found at el-Lāhūn, in the tomb of princess Sithathoriunet. Twelfth Dynasty

12 FILLET OF PRINCESS KHNUMET. Gold, cornelian, lapis lazuli and turquoise. Circumference 64 cm.; height of the upright motif 42 mm. Found at Dashūr in the tomb of princess Khnumet. Twelfth Dynasty

13 FILLET OF PRINCESS KHNUMET. Gold, cornelian, lapis lazuli and turquoise. Circumference 52 cm. Found at Dahshūr, in the tomb of princess Khnumet. Twelfth Dynasty

14 FILLET OF PRINCESS SITHATHORIUNET. Gold, cornelian, lapis lazuli and green felspar. Circumference 63.5 cm.; width of the gold band 28 mm. Found at el-Lahūn in the tomb of princess Sithathoriunet. Twelfth Dynasty

15 URAEUS. Gold, cornelian, lapis lazuli and green felspar or a pale green vitreous substance. Height 50 mm.; width 21 mm. Found at el-Lāhūn. Twelfth Dynasty

16 SCARAB RING. Gold, lapis lazuli, cornelian and green felspar. Length of the scarab 16 mm.; width 11 mm. Found at el-Lāhūn in the tomb of princess Sithathoriunet. Twelfth Dynasty

17a PENDANT. Gold and rock crystal. Diameter of the rosettes 24.5 mm.; of the medallion 21.5 mm. Found at Dahshūr in the tomb of princess Khnumet. Twelfth Dynasty

b NECKLACE. Gold. Length 28 cm. Found at Dahshūr in the tomb of princess Khnumet. Twelfth Dynasty

c NECKLACE FASTENING. Gold. Width 27 mm. Found at Dahshūr, in the tomb of princess Khnumet. Twelfth Dynasty

d NECKLACE WITH PENDANTS. Gold. Length 15.5 cm. Found at Dahshūr, in the tomb of princess Khnumet. Twelfth Dynasty

e LITTLE BIRDS. Gold. Height 11 mm. Found at Dahshūr, in the tomb of princess Khnumet. Twelfth Dynasty

18 NECKLACE. A modern reconstruction of single pieces found at Dahshūr, in the tomb of princess Khnumet. Gold, lapis lazuli, cornelian, turquoise and green felspar. Height of individual pieces 18—19 mm. Twelfth Dynasty

19 NECKLACE. Gold, lapis lazuli and turquoise. Diameter of the beads 7 mm.; height of the fastening 19.5 mm. A modern reconstruction of pieces found at Dahshūr, in the tomb of princess Mereret, replacing the less suitable earlier reconstruction of the pendants hanging from a string of large amethyst beads. Twelfth Dynasty

20 BELT (OR NECKLACE). Gold. Length of individual shells varies from 49—57 mm. Found at Dahshūr in the tomb of princess Mereret. Twelfth Dynasty

21a FRAGMENT OF A NECKLACE. Cornelian, lapis lazuli and green felspar. Length 80 mm. Found at Saqqāra. Twelfth Dynasty

b BRACELET. Gold, lapis lazuli and green felspar. Length 19 cm. Found at Saqqāra. Twelfth Dynasty

c NECKLACE. Gold, cornelian, green felspar and vitreous material (?). Length 33.5 cm. Found at Saqqāra. Twelfth Dynasty

d NECKLACE. Amethyst. Length 34 cm. Found at Saqqāra. Twelfth Dynasty

e NECKLACE. Cornelian. Length 41.5 cm. Found at Saqqāra. Twelfth Dynasty

f NECKLACE. Garnets and vitreous material (?). Length 30 cm. Found at Saqqāra. Twelfth Dynasty

22 PECTORAL OF KING AHMOSE. Gold, cornelian, lapis lazuli and turquoise. Height 72 mm.; width 92 mm. Found in 1859 in the tomb of queen Ahhotpe in Dra Abu el-Naga (Qurna). Early Eighteenth Dynasty

23 CHAIN WITH THREE FLY PENDANTS. Gold. Length of the chain 59 cm.; length of each fly 67 mm. From the treasure of queen Ahhotpe found in 1859. Early Eighteenth Dynasty

24 NECKLACE OF QUEEN AHHOTPE. Gold. Width 37.5 cm. From the queen's treasure, found in 1859. Early Eighteenth Dynasty

25 CROWN OF QUEEN AHHOTPE. Gold, cornelian, lapis lazuli and green felspar. Width 11 cm. Found in 1859, attached to the hair on the queen's mummy. Early Eighteenth Dynasty

26 BRACELET OF QUEEN AHHOTPE. Gold. Outer diameter 10.4 cm.; inner diameter 7.4 cm. Found in 1859. Early Eighteenth Dynasty

27 BRACELET OF QUEEN AHHOTPE. Gold, cornelian and lapis lazuli. Outer circumference 16.5 cm.; width 35 mm. Found in 1859. Early Eighteenth Dynasty

28 BRACELET OF QUEEN AHHOTPE. Gold, cornelian, lapis lazuli and an unidentified green stone or vitreous substance (?). Diameter 66 mm.; height of the vulture 73 mm. Found in 1859. Early Eighteenth Dynasty

29 AXE OF KING AHMOSE. Gold, electrum, cornelian, lapis lazuli and turquoise or a vitreous substance of similar appearance (?). Length of the whole axe 47.5 cm.; of the blade 13.4 cm. Found in 1859 in the tomb of queen Ahhotpe. Early Eighteenth Dynasty

30 AXE OF KING AHMOSE (Detail of plate 29)

31 EAR-RINGS. Alabaster and a coloured vitreous substance (?). Diameter of the larger disk 30.5 mm. Found at Saqqāra. New Kingdom

32 PECTORAL OF KING TUTANKHAMŪN. Gold, lapis lazuli, cornelian and glass. Height 65 mm.; width 11 cm. Found in Tutankhamūn's tomb. Late Eighteenth Dynasty

33 FASTENING (Detail of pectoral in plate 32) Gold, lapis lazuli, felspar, onyx, cornelian and green glass. Length 36 mm. Late Eighteenth Dynasty

34 PECTORAL IN THE SHAPE OF AN UDJAT EYE. Gold, lapis lazuli, an unidentified green stone and coloured glass. Height 57 mm.; width 95 mm. Found in Tutankhamūn's tomb. Late Eighteenth Dynasty

35 PECTORAL (Detail of plate 34)

36 PECTORAL WITH A WINGED SCARAB. Gold, silver, chalcedony, cornelian, lapis lazuli, calcite, obsidian (?) and red, black, green, blue and white glass. Height 14.9 cm.; width 14.5 cm. Found in Tutankhamūn's tomb. Late Eighteenth Dynasty

37 PECTORAL. Gold, cornelian, and blue and red glass. Height 16.5 cm.; width 24.4 cm. Found in Tutankhamūn's tomb. Late Eighteenth Dynasty

38 FASTENING (Detail of pectoral in plate 38)

39 PECTORAL IN THE SHAPE OF A WINGED SCARAB. Gold, lapis lazuli, cornelian and dark blue glass. Height 90 mm.; width 95 mm. Found in Tutankhamūn's tomb. Late Eighteenth Dynasty

40 PECTORAL IN THE SHAPE OF AN UDJAT EYE. Gold and blue faience. Height 60 mm.; width 88 mm. Found in Tutankhamūn's tomb. Late Eighteenth Dynasty

41 NECKLACE WITH PECTORAL. Gold, electrum, lapis lazuli, green felspar, calcite and glass. Height 11.8 cm.; width 10.8 cm. Found in Tutankhamūn's tomb. Late Eighteenth Dynasty

42 DJED PECTORAL. Gold, cornelian (or rock crystal set in red cement) and coloured glass. Height 12.0 cm.; width 16.3 cm. Found in Tutankhamūn's tomb. Late Eighteenth Dynasty

43 PECTORAL WITH THE GODDESS NUT. Gold, cornelian and coloured glass. Height 12.6 cm.; width 14.3 cm. Found in Tutankhamūn's tomb. Late Eighteenth Dynasty

44 PECTORAL IN THE SHAPE OF TUTANKHAMŪN'S FIRST NAME, NEBKHEPERURĒ. Gold, lapis lazuli, turquoise, cornelian, green felspar and calcite. Height 90 mm.; width 10.5 cm. Found in Tutankhamūn's tomb. Late Eighteenth Dynasty

45 COLLAR NECKLACE IN THE SHAPE OF THE VULTURE GODDESS NEKHBET. Gold and coloured glass. Height (including wings) 36.5 cm.; width (ditto) 46.5 cm. Found in Tutankhamūn's tomb. Late Eighteenth Dynasty

46 PECTORAL IN THE SHAPE OF A BA BIRD. Gold, turquoise, lapis lazuli and cornelian. Height 12.5 cm.; width 33 cm. Found in Tutankhamūn's tomb. Late Eighteenth Dynasty

47 HEAD OF TUTANKHAMŪN (Detail of pectoral in plate 46)

48 PECTORAL WITH A WINGED SCARAB. Gold, silver, electrum, lapis lazuli, cornelian, calcite, green felspar, obsidian (?) and white, blue, green and black glass. Height 12.5 cm.; width 13 cm. Found in Tutankhamūn's tomb. Late Eighteenth Dynasty

49 PECTORAL. Gold, cornelian (or rock crystal set in red cement), glass and greyish stone. Height 12.8 cm.; width 18.2 cm. Found in Tutankhamūn's tomb. Late Eighteenth Dynasty

50 PECTORAL SHAPED LIKE A FALCON. Gold, lapis lazuli, turquoise, cornelian, obsidian (?) and glass. Height 11.7 cm.; width 12.6 cm. Found in Tutankhamūn's tomb. Late Eighteenth Dynasty

51 PECTORAL OF OSIRIS. Gold, silver, cornelian (or rock crystal set in red cement) and glass. Height 15.5 cm.; width 20 cm. Found in Tutankhamūn's tomb. Late Eighteenth Dynasty

52 NECKLACE (or BRACELET?). Red and yellow gold and blue faience. Measurements not available. Found in Tutankhamūn's tomb. Late Eighteenth Dynasty

53 BRACELET. Gold, lapis lazuli, cornelian and turquoise. Length 15.5 cm.; width 4.6 cm. Found in Tutankhamūn's tomb. Late Eighteenth Dynasty

54 BRACELET. Gold, lapis lazuli, cornelian and turquoise. Diameter 54 mm. Found in Tutankhamūn's tomb. Late Eighteenth Dynasty

55 BRACELET. Gold, lapis lazuli, alabaster and turquoise coloured glass. Length of the whole bracelet 15.8 cm.; width 35 mm.; height of the scarab 66 mm. Found in Tutankhamūn's tomb. Late Eighteenth Dynasty

56 EAR-RINGS WITH PENDANTS. Gold, quartz, alabaster, coloured faience, and blue, white and green glass. Length 10.9 cm.; width 52 mm. Found in Tutankhamūn's tomb. Late Eighteenth Dynasty

57 EAR-RINGS WITH PENDANTS. Gold, cornelian, quartz, alabaster, coloured glass and faience. Length 10.9 cm.; width 52 mm. Found in Tutankhamūn's tomb. Late Eighteenth Dynasty

58 EAR-RINGS. Gold, cornelian and coloured glass. Length 70 mm. Found in Tutankhamūn's tomb. Late Eighteenth Dynasty

59 EAR-RINGS. Gold, resin and blue faience. Length 10 cm.; diameter 55 mm. Found in Tutankhamūn's tomb. Late Eighteenth Dynasty

60a RING. Gold. Diameter 18 mm.; bezel 18 × 15 mm. Found in Tutankhamūn's tomb. Late Eighteenth Dynasty

b RING. Gold and blue glass. Inner diameter 21 mm.; width of the ring 11 mm. Found in Tutankhamūn's tomb. Late Eighteenth Dynasty

c RING. Gold and dark blue, turquoise and red glass. Inner diameter 20 mm.; width of the ring at the broadest point, 14 mm. Found in Tutankhamūn's tomb. Late Eighteenth Dynasty

d RING. Gold. Inner diameter 22 mm.; width of the ring at the broadest point 7 mm. Found in Tutankhamūn's tomb. Late Eighteenth Dynasty

e RING. Gold and turquoise glass. Inner diameter 19 mm. Found in Tutankhamūn's tomb. Late Eighteenth Dynasty

61 RINGS (Another view of rings shown in plate 60a)

62 RING (Detail of ring 60b)

63 RING (Detail of ring 60c)

64 GOLD APPLIQUÉ ELEMENT. Red and yellow gold. Height 62 mm.; width 85 mm. Found in Tutankhamūn's tomb. Late Eighteenth Dynasty

65 GOLD APPLIQUÉ ELEMENT. Red and yellow gold. Measurements as for plate 64. Found in Tutankhamūn's tomb. Late Eighteenth Dynasty

66 GOLDEN THRONE OF TUTANKHAMŪN. Wood covered with gold lead, inlaid with gold and silver, coloured glass, faience and alabaster. Height 104 cm.; depth 64.5 cm.; width 53 cm. Found in Tutankhamūn's tomb. Late Eighteenth Dynasty

67 BACK OF TUTANKHAMŪN'S THRONE (Detail of plate 66)

68 NECKLACE. Gold and cornelian. Height 33 cm.; width 36 cm. Found at Tell Basta (Zagazig) in 1907. Nineteenth Dynasty

69 BRACELETS OF RAMESSES II. Gold and lapis lazuli. Diameter 56 mm.; width at the broadest point 59 mm. Found at Tell Basta (Zagazig). Nineteenth Dynasty

70 EAR-RINGS OF RAMESSES XI. Red gold. Length 16 cm.; width 53 mm. Found at Abydos. Twentieth Dynasty

71a RING. Gold and green schist. Length of the bezel 19 mm. New Kingdom

b RING. Gold and blue faience. Diameter 20 mm. New Kingdom

c RING. Gold and cornelian. Diameter 25 mm. Eighteenth Dynasty

d RING. Gold and steatite. Diameter 23 mm.. New Kingdom

72 PECTORAL. Gilt wood, resin, cornelian and glass. Height 11 cm.; width 14 cm. Found at Qurna in 1896. New Kingdom

73 PECTORAL (Reverse of the pectoral in plate 72)

74 PECTORAL OF KING PSIBKHENNĒ (PSUSENNES). Gold and semi-precious stones. Height 12 cm.; width 12 cm. Found in the royal necropolis at Tanis in 1940. Twenty-first Dynasty

75 PECTORAL OF KING PSIBKHENNĒ (PSUSENNES). Gold, semi-precious stones and coloured pebbles. Height 11 cm. Found in the royal necropolis at Tanis in 1940. Twenty-first Dynasty

76 PECTORAL OF KING HEKAKHEPERRĒ SHESHONQ. Gold, lapis lazuli, cornelian and glass. Width 78 mm. Found in the royal necropolis at Tanis in 1940. Twenty-second Dynasty

77a PENDANT. Gold. Height 109 mm. Found in the royal necropolis at Tanis in 1940. Twenty-first- Dynasty

b PENDANT. Gold. Height 93 mm. Found in the royal necropolis at Tanis in 1940. Twenty-first Dynasty

c PENDANT. Gold. Height 72 mm. Found in the roal necropolis at Tanis in 1940. Twenty-first Dynasty

78 BRACELET OF KING PSIBKHENNĒ (PSUSENNES). Gold and lapis lazuli. Length c. 21 cm.; width 35 mm. Found in the royal necropolis at Tanis, in 1940. Twenty-first Dynasty

79 BRACELET OF KING HEKAKHEPERRĒ SHESHONQ. Gold and semi-precious stones. Height 47 mm; diameter 65 mm. Found in the royal necropolis at Tanis in 1940. Twenty-second Dynasty

80 RING. Gold and semi-precious stones or glass. Height 18 mm. Found in the royal necropolis at Tanis in 1940. Twenty-first Dynasty

81 SHIELD FOR THE TOES OF THE MUMMY. Gold. Height 25 – 50 mm. Found in the tomb of king Psibkhennē (Psusennes) at Tanis. Twenty-first Dynasty

82 PLATE FOR COVERING THE ABDOMINAL INCISION IN THE MUMMY. Gold. 165 × 98 mm. Found in the coffin of king Psibkhennē (Psusennes) in 1940. Twenty-first Dynasty

83 BRACELET OF PINEDJEM. Gold, lapis lazuli and cornelian. Outer diameter 68 mm.; thickness 8 mm. Found in the tomb of the high priest Pinedjem in 1886. Twenty-first Dynasty

84a RING. Gold, lapis lazuli and cornelian. Width 20 mm. Found at Abusīr in 1888. Late Dynastic Period

b RING. Gold and semi-precious stones. Width, measured through the stones, 22 mm. Found at Saqqāra in 1893. Late Dynastic Period

85 MUMMY'S BEAD SHROUD. Gold, lapis lazuli, green felspar, faience and obsidian. Height 145 cm.; width 46 cm. Reconstructed from separate pieces found in the tomb of Tjanenhebu at Saqqāra. Twenty-sixth Dynasty

86 BRACELET. Gold. Distance from one head to the other 14.5 cm.; length of the spiral 60 mm.; width of the band 7 mm. Found in the eastern delta. Roman period, first century A.D.

87 BRACELET. Gold and beryls. Length of the spiral 76 mm.; width of the band 7 mm. Found at Sa el-Hagar (Sais) in 1906. Roman period, first century A.D.

88 RING. Gold. Diameter 21 mm.; width of the bezel 6 mm. Bought in 1893. Hellenistic period

89a BRACELET. Gold and agate. Longer diameter 65 mm.; thickness 8 mm.; bezel 25 × 22 mm. Found at Kom Abu Billo in 1903. Roman period, third century A.D.

  b BRACELET. Gold and agate. Longer diameter 80 mm.; thickness 10 mm.; bezel 36 × 35 mm. Found at Zagazig (Bubastis) in 1881. Roman period, thid century A.D.

90a RING. Gold and green jasper. Inner diameter 18 mm.; length of the bezel 19 mm. Found at Mit Rahina (Memphis) in 1903. Hellenistic period

  b RING. Gold and green jasper. Diameter 20 mm.; bezel 16 × 11 mm. Acquired by exchange in 1894. Hellenistic period

  c RING. Gold and lapis lazuli. Diameter 26 mm.; length of the bezel 19 mm. Hellenistic period

91 EAR-RINGS. Gold. Diameter 32 mm. Greek period, 3rd cent. B.C.

92 EAR-RINGS. Gold. Diameter 29 and 30 mm. Found at Abydos in 1881. Hellenistic period, third century B.C.

93 EAR-RINGS. Gold. Length 30 mm.; width 20 mm. Found at Mit Rahina (Memphis). Roman period

94 EAR-RING. Gold. Diameter 23 mm.; height of the basket 13 mm. Byzantine period